Schools Help Us Learn

Schools Help Us Learn

a building block book

Lee Sullivan Hill

Carolrhoda Books, Inc./Minneapolis

For my brother, Roger, with love and prayers—L. S. H.

The photographs in this book are reproduced through the courtesy of: Tony Stone Images: (© Jamey Stillings) front cover, (© Phil Schermeister) back cover and p. 20, (© Cathlyn Melloan) p. 2, (© Craig Blouin) p. 5, (© Lawrence Migdale) p. 6, (© Arthur Tilley) p. 10, (© Andy Sacks) p. 11, (© Kindra Clineff) p. 19, (© Chip Henderson) p. 22, (© Rene Sheret) p. 23, (© Robert E. Daemmrich) p. 25; © Diane C. Lyell, p. 1; © Steve Strickland, p. 7; © Images International/Bud Nielsen, p. 8; © Howard Ande, pp. 9, 21, 27; © Elaine Little/World Photo Images, pp. 13, 29; Dave Hanson/Minnesota Center for Arts Education, p. 14; © Steven Ferry/P&F Communications, p. 15; © Pat Wadecki/Root Resources, p. 16; Fanning/Howey Associates, Inc./Photography by Emery, pp. 12, 17, 24; © Richard B. Levine/Frances M. Roberts, p. 18; © Bob Firth/Firth Photobank, p. 26; © Dick Hemingway, p. 28.

Carolrhoda Books, Inc., c/o The Lerner Publishing Group
241 First Avenue North, Minneapolis, MN 55401 U.S.A.

Website address: www.lernerbooks.com

Library of Congress Cataloging-in-Publication Data

Hill, Lee Sullivan, 1958–
    Schools help us learn / Lee Sullivan Hill.
        p.   cm. — (A building block book)
    Includes index.
    Summary: Introduces various kinds of schools, their size and location, whether attended by children or adults, and the kinds of learning provided in each.
        ISBN 1-57505-092-7
        1. Schools—United States—Juvenile literature. 2. Education—United States—Juvenile literature. [1. Schools. 2. Education.]   I. Title. II. Series: Hill, Lee Sullivan, 1958– Building block book.
    LA210.H55   1998
    371'.00973—dc21
                                                                                    97-30741

Manufactured in the United States of America
1 2 3 4 5 6 – SP – 03 02 01 00 99 98

A yellow bus pulls up at school. Children
have come to learn. Do you ride a bus to school
or walk down city streets?

5

Inside, the school day begins. A teacher asks questions. Children wave their hands with answers. This classroom has a shiny floor and desks all in a row.

Other classrooms have wooden floors and benches. A metal roof keeps out the sun. Cool breezes float through open windows.

With so many different people and places,
there are all kinds of schools. Some schools
don't have walls—or a roof. Learn to ski at a
ski school, or take sailing lessons. Buildings
don't make a school. Learning does.

You can make the world your classroom on a field trip. Visit the fire station near your school. Or travel all the way to Washington, D.C. Take a picture of your class on the steps of the United States Capitol.

Why not bring the world into your classroom?
Computers let people send homework by E-mail
and study with teachers far away.

Sometimes school feels like home. If you are home-schooled, it really is home. Your mother and father might be your teachers.

What does your school look like? Is it a room
at home or a big brick building?

Does everyone dress differently? Or does everyone wear the same thing? At some schools, students wear uniforms. They don't have to decide what to wear every morning.

Magnet schools attract students who want to study something special. Young people who love to dance can take lessons every day at a magnet school for the arts.

At a school for the hearing impaired, children learn how to read lips and sign with their hands. Lights blink when it's time for recess because students might not hear a bell.

There are old schools that have been around
for years and years. Phillips Exeter Academy
opened in 1781.

And there are brand-new schools. Smell the
fresh paint at Dakota High School. You could
almost skate on the squeaky-clean floors.

In the city, school buildings must be big to fit so many children. Stone and brick rise up to the sky like a huge castle tower.

Schools are usually smaller in the country. Fewer children live nearby. A country school might look just like a house with a grassy yard and shady trees.

19

Schools are not only for children. Adults can learn to drive trucks or fix cars at trade schools. They can study at community colleges close to home or at colleges and universities far away.

At West Point, young men and women take
college classes in science and history. They also
learn to be leaders in the U.S. Army.

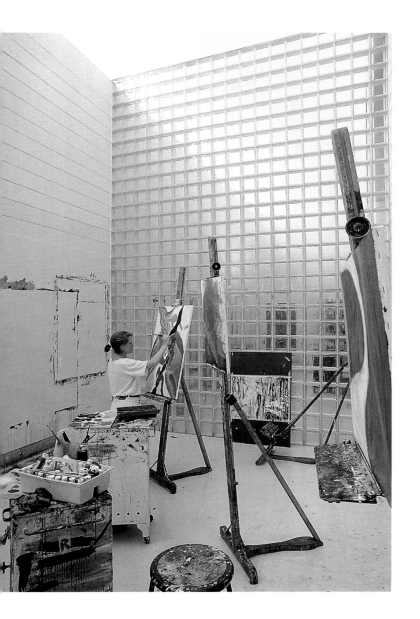

Some colleges teach people who love to draw and paint. Many of the students work as artists when they are done with school.

There are schools where people study cooking. Master chefs are the teachers. They share their skills with students who want to become chefs, too.

Schools are places where people share ideas.

Teachers help students solve problems.

Librarians teach children how to find books.

When you grow up, you could work at a
school. You could be a gym teacher and show
children how to stretch.

You could be an engineer and help build new schools.

Or you could drive a big yellow bus and bring children home at the end of the day.

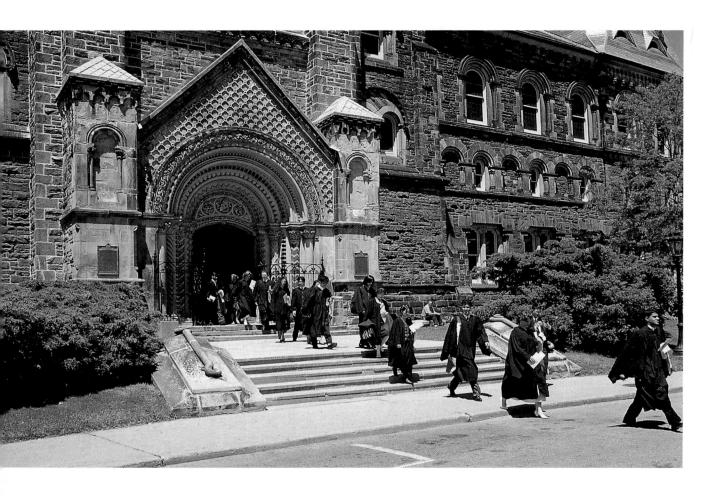

With all that you learn at school, you can
become whatever you like. Schools give us
the tools to keep on learning and growing.

Schools teach us about people and places
all over the world. Schools help us learn.

A Photo Index to the Schools in This Book

Cover The Walnut Grove School opened in 1863 on the Illinois prairie. It was replaced by a larger school in 1956.

Page 1 Kaichi Gakko is a museum of education that used to be a school. Built in 1876, it was the first modern elementary school in the central part of Japan.

Page 2 Woodburn Hall crowns a hill on the campus of West Virginia University. It was built in 1876. Imagine the view from one of the tower windows!

Page 5 Children in kindergarten through eighth grade ride a bus to this school in South Brewick, Maine.

Page 6 You can tell by the flag in the picture that this classroom is in the United States. These children start each day by saying the Pledge of Allegiance. How do you start the school day?

Page 7 Children in Poniensta, Ecuador, attend their village school. Older students help teach the younger children their lessons.

Page 8 The ski school at Mount Bachelor in Deschutes County, Oregon, has a whole mountain for its classroom.

Page 9 Do you recognize this building? It is the United States Capitol in Washington, D.C. Where would you like to go on a field trip?

Page 10 Computers are important tools in schools. Students create pictures and stories, look up facts, and use the Internet to learn about the world.

Page 11 A mother goes over a lesson with her daughter. Home-schooling lets children learn at their own pace. Sometimes students take art or gym classes at nearby public schools to round out their studies and meet other children.

 **Page 12** The school board in Indianapolis, Indiana, wanted to replace an old, crumbling schoolhouse. Architects and engineers planned a new school. Fanning/Howey Associates designed the new Washington Irving School, which opened in 1994.

 **Page 13** This school is in the Philippines. School uniforms are required in many parts of the world. In the United States, uniforms are usually worn only at private schools, but some public schools are experimenting with the idea.

 **Page 14** These students go to a public high school called the Minnesota Center for Arts Education. Many city school systems have magnet schools for arts, sciences, or languages.

 **Page 15** This student at a school for the deaf in England is wearing headphones to magnify sounds. Most hearing-impaired people can hear some sounds. With a teacher's help, the student is learning to speak.

 **Page 16** The Academy Building was built at Phillips Exeter in 1914. Back then, only boys studied at the private school in New Hampshire. It became coeducational (for both girls and boys) in 1971.

 **Page 17** Where do you think Dakota High School is located? It's not in North or South Dakota.... It's in Macomb, Michigan. Two thousand students go to this new school.

 **Page 18** This is P.S. 1 in New York City. The initials *P.* and *S.* stand for public school. Some cities use numbers instead of names to keep track of all the schools. (The school on page 12 uses both a name and a number.)

 **Page 19** Kindergarten classes meet at the Red Brick School in Franklin, Massachusetts. It is the oldest continually operated one-room school in the United States. The 1833 building replaced an even older wood-framed school built in 1792.

Page 20 Students come from all over the world to study at Harvard University. The school, founded in 1636, lies across the Charles River from Boston, Massachusetts.

Page 21 The United States Military Academy at West Point, New York, provides a free college education to bright students who agree to serve in the army after graduation. Famous Americans who went to West Point include Robert E. Lee, Ulysses S. Grant, and George S. Patton.

Page 22 This college student is creating a painting for her homework. She attends the University of North Carolina at Chapel Hill.

Page 23 Students take notes during a class at the California Culinary Academy in San Francisco, California. Do the students get to eat their homework after they are done?

Page 24 The library at Batesville Primary School in Indiana is a busy place. A volunteer checks out books while a librarian teaches a group of students.

Page 25 A gym teacher at Becker Elementary School in Austin, Texas, works with second graders. She teaches them how to keep strong and play fun games.

Page 26 Engineers are building a school in Eden Prairie, Minnesota. Crops of new homes sprouted up and brought new families, so the town needed another school.

Page 27 School bus drivers wait while students climb aboard on a snowy day in Sycamore, Illinois. Bus drivers go to driving school to learn how to steer the big buses around tight corners.

Page 28 Students march in robes on their way to the graduation ceremony. Their school, University College, is one of many colleges that make up the University of Toronto in Ontario, Canada.

Page 29 These children are on their way to school in Tokyo, Japan.

Willa Cather

Willa Cather

AUTHOR AND CRITIC

BETTINA LING

FRANKLIN WATTS
A Division of Scholastic Inc.
New York Toronto London Auckland Sydney
Mexico City New Delhi Hong Kong
Danbury, Connecticut

For Chuck
with love and thanks

Photographs © 2003: Art Institute of Chicago: 77 left (Jules Breton, French, 1827-1906, The Song of the Lark, oil on canvas, 1884, 110.6 x 85.8 cm, Henry Field Memorial Collection, 1894.1033); Beverly J. Cooper: 18, 20; Carnegie Library of Pittsburgh: 48, 49; Corbis Images: 23, 56, 58, 83, 90 (Bettmann), 14 (Raymond Gehman), 94 (Ron Watts); Getty Images/New York Times Co.: cover, back cover ghost; Historical Society of Western Pennsylvania, Pittsburgh, PA/Library and Archives Division: 54, 60; James M. Goble: 24; Nebraska State Historical Society/Willa Cather Pioneer Memorial Collection: 6, 8 right, 8 left, 12, 15, 27, 36, 44, 51, 89; Collection of the New-York Historical Society (#75609): 62; Omaha Public Library: 2; TimePix/Time Magazine: 95; University of Nebraska-Lincoln Libraries/Archives and Special Collections: 10, 30, 34, 41, 65, 66, 69, 77 right, 86, 98, 100.

Library of Congress Cataloging-in-Publication Data

Ling, Bettina.
  Willa Cather : author and critic / by Bettina Ling.
  p. cm. — (Great life stories)
Includes bibliographical references (p.) and indexes.

Contents: Virginia roots—The prairie world—Her own identity—A change of heart—Editor and critic—From journalism to teaching—The world of publishing—A writer finds her voice—New inspirations—Stories from the heart—A literary heritage—Final chapters—Timeline.

ISBN 0-531-12316-2

1. Cather, Willa, 1873–1947—Juvenile literature. 2. Novelists, American—20th century—Biography—Juvenile literature. 3. Critics—United States—Biography—Juvenile literature. [1. Cather, Willa, 1873–1947. 2. Authors, American. 3. Women—Biography.]   I. Title.   II. Series.

PS3505.A87Z726 2003
813'.52—dc21

2003004546

Contents

Willa Cather's original first name was Willela.
This photograph shows her as an infant.

Virginia Roots

American writer Willa Cather was born on December 7, 1873, in the state of Virginia. She was the daughter of Charles Fectigue Cather and Mary Virginia Boak Cather. Willa's parents were thrilled with the birth of their first child. They named her Willela after Charles's younger sister, who had died as a child.

The Cather family lived in Back Creek Valley, which is located near the city of Winchester in Virginia's Shenandoah Valley. Charles and Mary were both from large families that had lived in the region since the 1700s. Charles's great-grandfather and grandfather had both been farmers, as was his father, William Cather, who also served as a sheriff. Charles's mother, Caroline, was the daughter of a Back Creek tavern owner. Mary's grandfather had owned a mill in Back Creek, and her father had been an official in the government.

Willa's parents lived near each other as children, but only met when they were teenagers while attending the same school in Baltimore, Maryland. They fell in love, and a few years later were married on December 5, 1872. Charles was a friendly, compassionate young man. Tall, fair-haired, and handsome, he had kind blue eyes and a gentle smile. Before his marriage, Charles studied law for two years, but his first job was as deputy sheriff, serving alongside his father. Charles never practiced law, but often helped neighbors with their legal problems.

Mary Virginia (called Jennie by family and friends) had been a schoolteacher before she married, but devoted herself to taking care of Willa and running the household. She was an attractive woman with lots of energy and a strong personality. In the household Jennie ruled over Charles, who had an easygoing manner. She was also a very caring woman who always knew when a neighbor's child was ill or someone needed help.

Both of Willa's parents, Jennie and Charles Cather, grew up in the Back Creek Valley area.

Jennie and Charles were living with Jennie's mother, Rachel Boak, when Willa was born. A healthy baby, Willa grew quickly. At fourteen months old, she was walking and beginning to talk. In the fall of 1874, her parents moved to her grandfather Cather's farm when Charles's parents decided to visit their son George and his wife, Frances, who lived in Webster County, Nebraska. Willa's uncle had moved his family to Nebraska looking for better farming opportunities. William left Charles and Jennie in charge of the Cather farm. Grandma Rachel and her housekeeper, "Aunt Till," also came to live with Willa's family.

WILLOW SHADE MEMORIES

The Cather farm was named Willow Shade and was about 1 mile (1.6 kilometers) east of the village of Back Creek. It got its name from the many willow trees that surrounded it. Willow Shade and its surroundings

Virginia in the Late 1800s

In 1873, Back Creek Valley was a sparsely settled community of farms and small businesses located on a major roadway called the Northwest Turnpike. This period was less than a decade after the Civil War ended in 1865, and Virginia along with the rest of the South was still recovering from the devastation of that terrible conflict. Thousands of Virginian men had died in the war, and the state had been the scene of several major battles, many of which were fought in the Shenandoah Valley. Many farms and much property were destroyed. After the war and its destruction, many farming families moved to the West, looking for better farmland.

were at the center of Willa Cather's early memories. The main house was a large, three-story, red brick building with many rooms and lots of windows. There was also a smaller, white, wood farmhouse and a large barn. A stream spanned by a rustic bridge ran through the front yard, and crop fields and wildflower meadows were behind the buildings. When Charles took over his father's farm, he decided that sheep would be more profitable than raising crops, so Willow Shade became a sheep farm. A good businessman, Charles did well as a sheep farmer.

Willa was a bright, inquisitive little girl who loved to follow the adults as they did chores or visited with friends. She often accompanied her father when he went out at night to drive the sheep into their pens. Charles would scoop Willa up and carry her on his shoulders. She loved watching as her father and Old Vic, the family's sheepdog, rounded up the sheep. Willa later told an interviewer about how her father took good care of Old Vic. When the sheepdog cut its paws on the rocks in the fields, Charles made little leather shoes to protect Old Vic's feet.

Willa's love of nature began in her childhood days at Willow Shade, the Cather family farm.

Little Willa liked to be part of whatever was going on. When she was three years old, her parents took her along when they went ice-skating. They put Willa on a blanket so she could watch them as they skated. But she didn't want to just sit and watch and cried out to her mother and father, letting them know she wanted to skate too. Her father cut a branch from a pine tree, and pulled Willa across the ice on it so she could be part of the fun.

Charles's parents liked Nebraska and moved there permanently in 1877. That same year, Willa turned four and her mother gave birth to Willa's first brother, Roscoe. With her mother busy with the new baby, Willa spent a lot of time with her grandmother Rachel who introduced Willa to reading by teaching her from the Bible and other books.

Two of Willa's favorite books were *Pilgrim's Progress* by John Bunyan and *Universal History* by Peter Parley. The history stories in *Universal History* thrilled Willa, and she liked to imagine herself back in the different times in history. She loved to play for hours on a pretend chariot made by putting one chair upside down on top of another. Climbing on top, she'd sit silently and drive her chariot, daydreaming about her adventures in it.

Grandmother Rachel helped Willa learn her ABC's and helped her learn to read and write. Along with her love of stories, Willa liked to look at pictures and artwork. She was fascinated by the woodblock pictures in old books and inspected all the details in the family portraits hanging on the walls.

Willa's grandmother was a strong influence in her life. Those early years of reading with her probably gave Willa her lifelong love of books and reading. A short, rugged woman, Grandmother Rachel helped Willa learn home skills, such as sewing and quilting. Back Creek Valley women and girls had a long tradition of fine quilting. Willa's mother and both grandmothers were all quilters, and her great-aunt Sidney Gore was a well-known quilt maker in the region. Willa learned to piece, or put together, quilts at the age of five by watching the older women as they sat and quilted. It wasn't long before she began wanting to make her own quilt and was taught how to stitch. Willa would carefully select the fabric for her quilt and give special attention to her stitches.

One of Willa's favorite activities was sitting with her grandmother and Aunt Till in the kitchen as they sewed and talked. Willa would listen to their stories as she sewed her own small piece of patchwork. Quilting and storytelling were always part of her childhood memories.

CHILDHOOD ADVENTURES

Willa's life at Willow Shade was exciting at times. One of her most memorable childhood events happened when she was about five or six years old, and involved her grandmother Rachel and Aunt Till, who had been with the Boak family since Willa's

Grandmother Rachel was an important figure in young Willa's life. She helped Willa learn to read and exposed her to many wonderful books.

grandmother was a little girl. Although she was a free woman by the time Willa knew her, Aunt Till had been a slave for most of her life. She had a daughter, Nancy, who was born before slavery was outlawed. Grandmother Rachel had helped Nancy escape to freedom in Canada, and Aunt Till had not seen her daughter since the escape twenty-five years earlier.

Willa had heard the story of Nancy Till's escape many times. Her mother made up a lullaby about it and used it to sing little Willa to sleep. So when Nancy was finally able to come home to see her mother after all those years away, young Willa was as excited as the adults. She was with Aunt Till the day Nancy arrived and witnessed the joyous scene as mother and daughter rushed into each other's arms, embracing after so many years apart. Later, Willa listened as Nancy, Aunt Till, and Grandmother Rachel sat in the kitchen and discussed everything that had happened since Nancy's journey to Canada. The memory of that day was so emotionally powerful for Willa that she never forgot it, and sixty-four years later, she would use it in her last novel.

As Roscoe—called Ross by the family—grew older, he and Willa became very close pals and spent long hours playing together. Willow Shade was a wonderful place in which to be a child. The big house had plenty of places to play hide-and-seek, and the sheep barn contained a hayloft where the siblings would play for hours at a time. Sometimes the children walked the short distance down the road to visit the nearby mill and mill house where their great-grandfather had been the miller and Grandmother Rachel had grown up.

Willa loved to roam the woods and fields around Willow Shade, sometimes with Ross, but often by herself. She'd spend hours looking at the different trees and shrubs, and picking wildflowers such as jonquils, lilacs, morning glories, azaleas, and wild honeysuckles, and dogwood blossoms. These early years spent playing in the woods gave Willa a deep love and respect for nature that she carried with her for the rest of her life.

LISTENING TO STORIES AND TALES

One of Willa's favorite places in the house was the warm, inviting kitchen. It contained three big tables—one for making bread, another for pastry, and a third for cutting up meat—and floor-to-ceiling cupboards for storing sugar, spices, and other goods. There was always something cooking in the kitchen, either on the big stove or in the huge fireplace that had a crane to lift heavy cooking pots into and out of the fire. Willa would watch as bread was made, butter was churned, or jars of fruit preserves were prepared.

The fields and woods provided endless hours of entertainment for Willa.

During the winter evenings, the house staff sat around the kitchen fireplace, talking and cracking nuts. Sometimes Willa got to stay up late and hear their exciting stories. Often, the talk was about the Civil War. Many of the men in Back Creek had fought in the war, including some of Willa's uncles. One story Willa heard was about her uncle William Boak, who had died fighting in a famous Civil War battle. The story so moved the imaginative young girl that she changed her name in the family Bible from Willela to William, insisting she was named after her uncle. The family gave her the nickname of "Willie."

The Cather household was a busy place, and there was always something interesting going on. In 1880, another baby, Douglass, was born, and in 1881, sister Jessica joined the family. Visitors came and went, as Willa's parents often entertained relatives or friends from Winchester. Willa and her siblings enjoyed all the company and were particularly pleased when salesmen, such as

Willa was particularly close to her brothers, Roscoe (left) and Douglass (right).

the broom maker, Uncle Billy Parks, came to the house. It was fun to see what was for sale or watch Uncle Billy fix a broom.

Willa and her brothers and sister were healthy children and didn't have any serious illnesses during childhood, except the usual colds during the winters. Sometimes, when the Cather house was very busy and one of the children was sick, Willa's parents would ask a neighbor named Mary Ann Anderson to come in and watch over the sick child. Mrs. Anderson often brought along her daughter, Marjorie. Although born with limited intelligence, Margie was sweet and fun, and Willa liked her very much. She was always happy when Mrs. Anderson and Margie came to the house.

Margie eventually came to work at Willow Shade as a housemaid. Though older than Willa, she became one of Willa's favorite companions. The girls strolled the woods and fields, and took walks up the nearby country road to visit Margie's mother and hear her folktales about the region.

Mary Love was another childhood friend of Willa's. Mary was about the same age as Willa and the girls played at each other's houses. Mary's mother had been educated in France and liked to talk about her experiences in that country. Mrs. Love's stories must have made an impression on the young Willa. When she grew up, one of the first European countries Willa visited was France.

The stories Willa heard during this period of her childhood—the servants' tales, Nancy Till's story, Mrs. Anderson's folktales, and Mrs. Love's stories about France—all stayed with the young, imaginative girl and would inspire her to write stories of her own.

LOOKING TOWARD A NEW PLACE

The Cather family members who were living in Nebraska had been writing to Charles and urging him to bring his family and join them out West. George Cather wrote about the good farming and the dry prairies—a healthy place for anyone with lung problems. Some members of the Cather family, including four great-uncles and two aunts of Willa, had developed tuberculosis, a disease of the lungs. It was possible that Charles or his children might also get the disease one day, and the dry Nebraska prairie would be a better place to live than the in moist climate of Virginia.

Charles made the trip to Nebraska to see for himself what life was like out there, and after hard thinking, he decided his family should also move to Nebraska. In February of 1883, he auctioned off his farm and

Nebraska Settlement

Midway between the Atlantic and Pacific Oceans, Nebraska is part of an enormous 500-mile (804.5-km) plain that stretches between the Missouri River and the Rocky Mountains. A major overland route, the Oregon Trail, ran through Nebraska and was used beginning in the early 1800s by settlers, fur traders, gold miners, and explorers on their journeys west. After the U.S. Congress passed the Homestead Act of 1862, which gave settlers 160 acres (395.2 hectares) of free land if they agreed to live on the land and farm it for five years, large numbers of settlers from eastern and southern states and European immigrants moved to Nebraska.

equipment, and the family got ready to leave Virginia. Along with Charles, Jennie, and their children, Grandmother Rachel, Margie Anderson and her brother, and two Boak cousins would be moving to the West.

Willa was very sad that her family was moving away from Willow Shade and Back Creek Valley. The nine-year-old did not want to leave her friends and relatives in the area or the woods and fields she'd spent hours exploring. Even Old Vic, the family sheepdog, would not be going with them. He'd been given to a neighbor. This move was the beginning of what would be a difficult period for the young girl.

The Cathers thought Nebraska would be a healthier place for the family to live.

The Prairie World

The Cather family traveled by train to the town of Red Cloud. They arrived in April of 1883 and were met at the train station by farmhands and wagons from Grandfather Cather's farm. There was more traveling to do since both William and George Cathers' farms were located about 12 miles (19.3 km) or so from Red Cloud. George owned 360 acres (145.8 ha) of land for his home and farm. Willa's grandparents had settled on some of George's land about 2 miles (3.2 km) away from his farm. A number of other settlers lived in the area around the Cathers. There were enough people that the area was considered a small, separate township called Catherton (named by George).

As Willa rode in the back of a farm wagon, the countryside she saw shocked her. Gone were the familiar mountains, dense forests, waterfalls, and green wildflower meadows she knew from Virginia. Instead, there was only flat land and shaggy prairie grass that went on as far as the eye could see.

Catherton was located on a 70-mile (112.6 km)-long plateau of 0.5-mile (0.8 km)-wide land that divided the streams flowing south to the Republican River and those flowing north to the Little Blue River. Called the Divide, the plateau crossed northern Webster County and was

The Cather family arrived at the Red Cloud train station in April of 1883.

about 300 feet (91.4 meters) higher than the Republican River Valley. There were no other rivers or large bodies of water on the Divide. To the young girl who had spent the first nine years of her life growing up in Virginia's green, rolling fields crossed by its many rivers and streams, the stark contrast was deeply disturbing to her senses. In an interview Willa gave as an adult, she said the Nebraska countryside was "mostly wild pasture and as naked as the back of your hand." She told another interviewer, "As we drove further and further out into the country, I felt a good deal as if we had come to the end of everything."

HOMESICK FOR WILLOW SHADE

When the family arrived at her grandfather's farm, Willa was in for more shock. Grandfather William's simple, two-story farmhouse wasn't anything like big, lovely Willow Shade. The weathered wood-frame building had all the bedrooms and the living room on one floor and a kitchen and dining room in a basementlike area below.

The outside property contained a small vegetable garden, a barn, some storage buildings, a muddy pond, and cornfields. There were no plants or trees shading the house as the willows did in Virginia, but just a few thin ash tree seedlings that were barely surviving. The barns and other buildings were all weathered to the same dull gray. The farmyard was muddy and gray, and beyond were endless acres of prairie. The closest river or stream was miles away.

It was all so different from Virginia. Willa thought the land and everything she saw was ugly. She later told an interviewer that during that period, "I was little and homesick and lonely." These emotions of feeling displaced and homesick were so strong that they stayed with her for the rest of her life and became a theme in some of her stories.

During her first summer in Nebraska, Willa explored the countryside. Grandfather William had returned to Virginia to visit friends, and Grandmother Catherine had gone to live with George and his family. Willa's father took over running the farm. Her mother was in bed, sick after suffering a miscarriage, which left Grandmother Rachel and Margie to do the household chores. With Willa's mother in bed and her father and the other adults busy with farm chores, Willa and her brothers were free to roam the countryside, either on foot or on horseback.

Hungry to see something besides prairie grass, Willa and her brothers took long rides on horseback, looking for more plants or flowers. They discovered a small stream many miles from their farm with a few scrawny cottonwood and dwarf elm trees growing on its banks, and Willa later found a neighbor's small grove of broad-leafed catalpa trees and another neighbor's row of poplar trees. Willa returned again and again to look at the trees. In a scene in her novel *My Ántonia*, Willa uses one of her characters to give a voice to what she felt about the trees on the Nebraska landscape: "Trees were so rare in that country, and they had to make such a hard fight to grow, that we used to feel anxious about them, and visit them as if they were persons."

During that first year, Willa began to find more beauty in the Nebraska landscape. The tall prairie grass was full of quail and wild birds, and small, furry mammals known as prairie dogs lived in large underground burrows on the plains. The flat land made the bright blue skies look huge. There were many different varieties of wildflowers, such as bright yellow sunflowers, growing near shallow pools of water alongside the old trails.

As Willa explored the countryside, she met the other farm families that lived in Catherton. Most of the families who lived on the farms were immigrants from other countries. There were many Germans, Swedes, Danes, Norwegians, Bohemians (a country now part of the Czech Republic), and Czechs, and a few Russians, French, and Swiss. The nearest neighbors were a German family named Lambrecht, whose children became Willa's first Nebraska playmates.

Many people immigrated to the Red Cloud area from different parts of Europe, such as Germany and Norway. They hoped to find a better life for themselves and their families working the land.

Nebraska's Immigrants

The late 1800s was a time when many people immigrated to the United States. Large numbers of immigrants from the nations of central, eastern, and southern Europe, looking to escape from economic hardships and political and religious persecution in their countries, came to the United States looking for a better life. Many German, Czech, Swedish, Danish, Norwegian, and Russian immigrants settled in Nebraska to farm.

Willa was fascinated by the foreign speech and customs of the Europeans. She especially liked the old women in the families who told her stories about their home countries. In a 1913 interview, she said, ". . . . these old women on the farms were the first people who ever gave me the real feeling of an older world across the sea. Even though they spoke very little English, the old women somehow managed to tell me a great many stories about the old country. . . ." Willa felt a bond with them. They understood her homesickness, because they were also lonely for the homelands they had left behind. Willa found their stories exciting and committed them to her developing writer's memory.

In autumn of 1883, Willa attended class in a nearby one-room school. The school term lasted only three months, before winter snows made it too hard for Willa and the other children in the area to get to the school. Although she was not quite ten years old, Willa was extremely intelligent and way ahead of her age level in reading. Willa's parents were educated and liked to read, and the family bookcase contained many books and magazines. There were volumes of Shakespeare's plays, anthologies of poetry, and the works of great authors such as Charles Dickens,

Nathaniel Hawthorne, and Edgar Allan Poe. Willa read them all, while also devouring children's adventure books such as *The Swiss Family Robinson* and *The Adventures of Huckleberry Finn*.

Although Willa was warming up to the Nebraska landscape, it would be a while before she truly felt at home in the state. The first Christmas there was not a happy time for her. There were no beautiful pine trees to cut for a Christmas tree, and memories of wonderful Christmases back in Virginia made her homesick for the South.

Willa found Christmas time in Nebraska to be barren and bleak compared to the holidays back home in Virginia. She missed the beautiful pine trees that made great Christmas trees.

LIFE IN RED CLOUD

Willa's family lived on the farm until the fall of 1884, when Charles Cather gave up farming and decided to move the family to Red Cloud. Charles didn't really like farming, and Jennie was unhappy on the isolated farm, with the nearest neighbors so far away. Willa's parents also wanted their children to be able to attend a larger school.

Charles sold his animals and farm equipment, and the family moved into a small house in the center of Red Cloud, a town founded in 1871 and named for a Native American who was an Oglala Sioux chief. For Willa and her family, it was a very different place from the farms in Catherton and the quiet countryside.

Located just 6 miles (9.7 km) from the Kansas border, Red Cloud was a busy town of more than two thousand people. Two major railroads passed through it on routes that connected the town to Kansas City and Denver. Six to eight passenger trains a day stopped at the Red Cloud train station, which sat next to the Republican River 1 mile (1.6 km) south of the one main business street. The town had stores, a lumber mill, a cheese plant, a newspaper, banks, a schoolhouse, a courthouse, and several churches.

Red Cloud's side streets were laid out in neat rows of small houses with white fences and pretty yards. Young trees lined the wooden sidewalks. The Cathers' house was on a corner lot and was surrounded by a large yard with trees. It was just a block away from the main business section. Red Cloud was growing rapidly so housing was scarce, and Willa's father could find only a small house that cramped the large family.

Downstairs, there were a sitting room, dining room, kitchen, and bedrooms for Willa's parents, the younger children, and other adults. Up a narrow stairway from the kitchen was a large, unfinished attic, where Willa and her brothers lived in a kind of dormitory. It ran the whole length of the house, and the children loved it because it was their own private world away from adults.

The first summer in Red Cloud was a busy time for all the Cathers. Willa's father opened an office where he sold real estate, insurance, and offered farm loans. The family quickly made friends with neighbors and townspeople, including Silas and Lyra Garber. Silas, the founder of Red Cloud, had once served as governor of Nebraska. He and Lyra lived in a huge house on the outskirts of town, where they held picnics for friends in their beautiful cottonwood grove. Willa enjoyed visiting the Garbers, especially Lyra. She later wrote about both Lyra and Silas in one of her books.

Willa loved to explore the countryside with Ross, canoeing with him on the Republican River or riding out to Catherton to visit the farm families. Although Willa had been taught domestic skills, such as cooking

This photograph shows the Cather house in Red Cloud.

and sewing, she tried not to be a girl. A tomboy at heart, she liked riding, climbing, and fishing. Friends and family still called her "Willie."

The Cather children loved to go to the Republican River to see the Chalk Cliffs—beautiful exposed bluffs that rose dramatically above the river. Another favorite spot at the river was a place all the children in the region visited. Called Far Island, it was an oval sandbar, about 0.5 miles (0.8 km) long and 100 yards (91.4 m) wide. Willa and Ross liked to play treasure hunt with brother Douglass and their friends, acting out the pirate characters from one of their favorite books, *Treasure Island*. Willa later described Far Island in one of her short stories: "The island is known chiefly to the children who dwell in that region, and generation after generation of them have claimed it; fished there, and pitched their tents under the great arched tree, and built camp fires on its level, sandy outskirts."

During her first year in Red Cloud, eleven-year-old Willa attended South Ward School, where she produced one of her first pieces of writing, an essay about dogs and cats. At school, Willa made new friends quickly. A classmate, Margie Miner, and her family lived near the Cathers. Margie had two sisters, Carrie and Irene, who became Willa's lifelong friends. Mr. Miner owned the general store, and Mrs. Miner was an accomplished pianist from Norway. Willa enjoyed listening as Mrs. Miner played her beautiful grand piano. This was Willa's first time hearing classical music. Her great passion for music began during those visits to the Miner house.

At the Miner house, Willa met Anna Sadilek, who worked there as a housemaid. Anna, who was a few years older than Willa, and her family had come to Nebraska from Bohemia, hoping to find a better life. The Sadileks lived near the Cather farm in Catherton, but Willa had not met Anna until she saw her at the Miner house. An admirer of the strong immigrant women from the farms, Willa liked Anna immediately, and they became friends.

One of the first stories Willa heard when her family moved to Nebraska was about Anna's father's suicide, a powerful memory that stayed with Willa for years. Anna Sadilek would have a difficult life in the years to come, and Willa later used the details of Anna's life and her father's death as the basis of some stories and a book.

DISCOVERING THE ARTS

During her second year of school in Red Cloud, Willa's teacher was Eva King. King recognized that Willa was a talented, bright student and encouraged her studies. Willa's reading fueled her imaginative mind and helped shape her views of the world. She was reading translations of Latin and Greek classics, religious books, books on the Civil War, romance novels, dramatic plays, newspapers, and copies of ladies' and literary magazines.

The dramatic plays she read sparked an interest in the theater. As soon as the family moved into Red Cloud, Willa began to take part in amateur plays at the Baptist church her family attended. One of her best performances was as the Native American heroine Hiawatha. Willa made her own costume, complete with a bow and arrows.

In 1885, a new opera house had opened in Red Cloud and became a special place for Willa. During the winter, theatrical and musical traveling companies performed there. She loved watching the live performances and was inspired and influenced by the actors and actresses in the

Willa is shown here at the age of nine. Willa was a bright, imaginative child.

traveling stock companies. Willa tried to see as many performances as she could when a company was in town. Years later, in a letter to the editor of the *Omaha World-Herald*, she recalled those days, saying, "Only a living human being, in some sort of rapport with us, speaking the lines, can make us forget who we are and where we are, can make us (especially children) actually live in the story that is going on before us."

The theatrical productions at the opera house inspired the children of Red Cloud to put on their own shows. Willa liked to play boys' parts. When Willa and the Miner girls staged *Beauty and the Beast*, the Miner girls played the parts of Beauty and of the Beast while Willa played the merchant-father, dressed in a suit, hat, and waxed mustache.

Also around this time, Willa got her first taste of the political world. Willa's father was part of the Red Cloud town council, and Willa and her friends witnessed firsthand what happens when there's a disagreement between citizens and their town council. The children were inspired to create their own version of local government and built a play town in the Cather backyard. They called it "Sandy Point." Willa was elected mayor and was also editor of their newspaper, *The Sandy Point News.*

In 1886, as Willa turned thirteen, her brother James was born. Willa was entering her teen years and asked for her own bedroom, apart from her younger brothers and sister. Like many teenagers, she wanted a private space that was all hers, where she could read and be alone with her thoughts and dreams. Her parents partitioned off one end of the main attic under the gables of the roof. It had low ceilings that sloped down on either side and a large window that went to the floor.

Touring Red Cloud

Many sites in Red Cloud have been restored and preserved by the Willa Cather Pioneer Memorial and Educational Foundation. The western half of Webster County, where the Cather farms were located, was officially proclaimed as "Catherland" by the Nebraska State Legislature in 1965. In 1978, the properties in Red Cloud were given to the state of Nebraska to be administered as the Willa Cather Historical Center by the Nebraska State Historical Society. In 1980, an area of Red Cloud called the Willa Cather Thematic District was listed in the National Register of Historic Places. Willa's family home still stands in Red Cloud, and visitors can see Willa's attic bedroom with its original rose wallpaper still on the walls.

This little bedroom was Willa's own special world. She surrounded herself with her books and carefully selected each decorative object and picture. She covered the walls with wallpaper that had red and brown roses on a yellowish background. Willa got the paper herself by working in the local drugstore and taking the wallpaper instead of payment.

THREE

Her Own Identity

By the time she entered her teen years, Willa was an independent young woman. She adopted a middle name for herself, taking her grandmother Rachel's maiden name of Seibert, but changing the spelling to Sibert. Still a tomboy, she related much more to the strong immigrant farm women than she did to the delicate ladies from the town.

Willa's thinking translated into how she dressed. An attractive young woman with rosy skin and striking gray-blue eyes, she kept her reddish-brown hair cut short and wore shirts and ties with her skirts, and even sometimes wore a man's hat and carried a cane. She occasionally signed her name William Cather, Jr. She expressed contempt for the cumbersome clothing women were expected to wear.

This photograph was taken in the summer of 1890. Willa (right) is shown here with two friends, Margie Miner (left) and Eveleva Brodstone. Notice Willa's daring short haircut.

Although Willa's style of dressing may have set her apart from the "proper young ladies" of Red Cloud, it wasn't totally out of keeping with some women at the time she was growing up. There were famous actresses in the theater world at that time who dressed in men's clothing and played young male parts. Outside of the theater, some women's fashions were patterned after men's clothing, with stiff collars and cuffs on blouses, and ties.

Although Jennie Cather, a "proper Southern lady," hated the way Willa looked, both she and Willa's father indulged the young girl. Jennie believed in allowing all her children to be individuals. She knew Willa needed to develop in her own way.

Willa entered Red Cloud High School and was hungry to learn, whether it be inside or outside the classroom. At high school, two of her teachers, Mr. and Mrs. A. K. Goudy, noticed right away that Willa was different from the other students and helped her in subjects she had trouble with, such as spelling and math. They were influential in encouraging her to go to college, something that most young Red Cloud women—and men—did not do in those days.

Throughout high school, Willa was busy and involved with her studies and friends. She loved music and attending the musical plays performed at the Red Cloud Opera House. Although Willa liked to hear music, she never played an instrument, even though her mother hired a German music teacher to give Willa piano lessons. She had no interest in learning to play the piano because music was an emotional release for her, not something she wanted to perform.

A Changing Time for Women

The 1800s was a period of change for American women. In the 1700s, managing the home and family was the primary role of women. By the mid-1800s, married women were getting more education and involving themselves in health issues, women's rights, child labor, and other public policy issues. More young women were working outside the home as nurses, secretaries, and store clerks. This change was reflected in fashion. Women were abandoning the styles worn in the Victorian period of the 1800s—heavy, bulky outfits, stiff corsets (an undergarment that pulled in a woman's waist very tightly), and tight, pointy shoes—for lighter-weight fabrics, less confining clothing, and more comfortable shoes.

EDUCATION IN MANY PLACES

Willa continued her education even when she wasn't in school. She enjoyed being with adults because she learned so many things about the world from them. Willa had a number of adult friends, including the two

Willa takes a break during an outdoor outing and poses for a photograph with some of her friends and siblings. In the front row, there are, from left to right, Frances and Ellen Gere, Jessica Cather, Margie Miner, and Douglass Cather. In the back row, from left to right, there are Irene Miner, and Elsie, Willa, and Roscoe Cather.

doctors who practiced in Red Cloud. They often allowed her to ride along on their calls to patient's homes. Willa admired both men and loved to talk over their cases with them. The time she spent with the doctors influenced Willa so much that she was determined to become a doctor or scientist when she grew up.

When Willa wanted to study Latin, a language she loved, she struck up a friendship with an educated Englishman who lived in Red Cloud. He guided her in the study of Latin and also began teaching her Greek. The two read Greek and Latin classics and had long talks about religion, life, and death.

Willa also made friends with the Wieners, a Jewish European couple who lived around the corner from her house. They both spoke French and German and introduced Willa to translations of French and German literature. The Wieners gave Willa the run of their large library of books, and she saw fine artwork for the first time in the beautiful paintings on the walls of their home.

Willa graduated from high school in June of 1890 at the age of sixteen. Her graduating class consisted of only three students—Willa and two boys. This was the second graduating class at Red Cloud High School. Out of the three graduates, Willa was the only one who wanted to go on to college to further her education. When the graduates were asked to give graduation speeches, Willa was nervous but delivered an impressive speech entitled "Superstition versus Investigation." It was a strong defense of scientific research, and the Red Cloud newspaper published it. The following lines from the speech show that she was a deep thinker for a teenager: "Scientific investigation is the hope of our age, as it must precede all progress; and yet upon every hand we hear the objections to its pursuit. . . . Nevertheless, if we bar our novices from advancement, whence shall come our experts?"

Although Willa wanted to attend college, finding the money to finance her education was not easy. Charles Cather wasn't a wealthy man and didn't have the money for Willa's college education. He still had younger children to support, including a new Cather baby, Elsie. But Willa's parents knew how much their bright daughter wanted a college education, so Charles borrowed money from a business associate.

Willa wanted to attend the University of Nebraska, but found she would have to take some extra classes she'd not received at Red Cloud High School to meet all the requirements needed for acceptance to the school. The university ran a preparatory school called the Latin Preparatory School, where Willa could get the required classes. She'd have to go for one year before being allowed to enter the university as a freshman. In September of 1890, Willa and her mother set off for Lincoln, the capital of Nebraska and home of the University of Nebraska. She was about to enter an exciting new period of her life.

Red Cloud, The Plains, and Stories

Red Cloud, the Nebraska plains, and its people had an enormous effect on Willa Cather's writing. Six of her novels and several of her short stories are set in Red Cloud and Webster County. The town of Red Cloud served as the model for many of her fictional towns, and she patterned many characters in her books and stories after Red Cloud citizens.

FOUR

A Change of Heart

Lincoln, Nebraska, was eighteen times the size of Red Cloud and the first big city Willa had seen. It had a skyscraper (a six-story building), five large hotels, many different kinds of churches, five private schools, a public library, and an electric-light plant.

The buildings and campus of the University of Nebraska took up four city blocks, and it had a student population of about three or four hundred. Willa and her mother stayed with family friends until Willa found two rooms to rent in the rooming house of another friend. Her mother returned home, and Willa was on her own for the first time in her life. She was a self-sufficient young woman who was determined to succeed and excited about going to college.

Still intent on studying medicine and becoming a doctor, Willa began her studies at the Latin Preparatory School. She was given permission to take freshman chemistry along with the courses she needed to enter the university. Always a hard worker, Willa tackled her class work with energy and determination, sometimes getting up at five o'clock in the morning for extra studying.

CHANGING COURSE

In March of 1891, during her year at the Latin Preparatory School, Willa Cather experienced a life-changing event. In an English course taught by Professor Ebenezer Hunt, Willa wrote a paper on an essayist named Thomas Carlyle. Her passionate essay about Carlyle so impressed Professor Hunt he sent it to the *Nebraska State Journal* newspaper without Willa's knowledge.

On a Sunday morning soon afterward, Willa opened the *Journal* and found her essay in print. It was such an electrifying experience for the seventeen-year-old that it transformed her life. Many years later Willa said this about seeing her first words in print: "Up to that time I had planned to specialize in science; I thought I would like to study medicine. But what youthful vanity can be unaffected by the sight of itself in print! It has a kind of hypnotic effect. . . ."

That powerful effect caused her to change her career plans completely, switching from science and medicine to writing. Although she continued to take courses in botany and chemistry, it was English and literature she focused on. A light had turned on inside. She wanted to be a writer.

After finishing her preparatory courses, Willa began her freshman year of college in the fall of 1891. She took math, Greek, Latin, speech, and was allowed to enroll in a junior-level Shakespeare course. She also joined the staff of the college literary publication, *The Hesperian*.

During Willa's freshman year, she developed a close relationship with an English teacher and writer named Herbert Bates. Professor Bates gave Willa the kind of encouragement she needed as a writer. It

Willa joined the staff of *The Hesperian*, a literary publication at the University of Nebraska.

was in his English class that she began to write her fictional pieces. One of her stories so impressed Professor Bates that he sent it off to a Boston magazine, which published it in May of 1892. Entitled "Peter," it was the story Willa had heard about the suicide of Anna Sadilek's father. Professor Bates urged Willa to continue seriously studying the writing process.

During her college years, Willa was a brilliant student, taking courses in Latin, Greek, French, German, Shakespeare, Elizabethan dramatists, American and European history, dramatization, and philosophy. She did a year's study of the poet Robert Browning's work and of the works of other writers, such as Alfred Tennyson, Ralph Waldo Emerson, and Nathaniel Hawthorne.

Willa immersed herself in her studies of literature, language, and history during her time at University of Nebraska. She is shown here on the university campus in 1894.

SELECTIVE FRIENDSHIPS

Willa was as much an individualist in college as she'd been in high school, still wearing distinctive clothing such as suspenders, shirts and ties with her skirts. She was very outspoken and had no problem expressing her opinions about subjects even if they offended people. Because of her individuality, outspoken manner, and strong personality, Willa's classmates either really liked her or couldn't stand her.

During her college years, Willa wrote to an old teacher, Mrs. Goudy. Her letters revealed that inside, Willa wasn't as confident as she appeared to be. She questioned about who she was and felt lonely and was unhappy when people criticized her. Underneath her independence and nonconformity there was still a desire to be liked.

Willa did make some close friendships in college. Two students who became good friends were Mariel Gere and Louise Pound. Willa admired Gere's parents. Her father was the founder and editor of the *Nebraska State Journal*, and Gere's mother was a feminine, gracious woman who had a powerful sense of self. After spending time around Mrs. Gere, Willa began to modify her appearance and behavior somewhat, letting her hair grow longer and dressing in more feminine clothing.

Willa met Louise Pound when they both were associate editors of a college literary magazine. Pound was beautiful and known for her skills as a writer, athlete, pianist, and campus leader. Willa shared a love of learning with Pound, who would later became a famous scholar and folklorist. Along with writing and editing, they both took part in dramatic productions. Willa grew to love Pound very much. It was her deepest friendship in college.

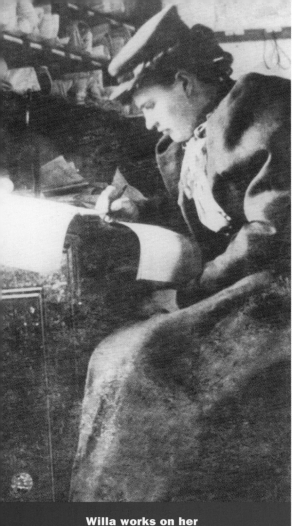

Willa works on her column for the *Nebraska State Journal* in their offices.

Along with student friendships, Willa formed close ties with a number of families, in particular, the Canfields. James Canfield was the chancellor of the university, and his wife, Flavia, was a painter who shared Willa's love of art, literature, and music. They had a daughter, Dorothy, who was a few years younger than Willa. Dorothy Canfield also loved the arts, especially books and writing. Willa and Dorothy became close friends and their friendship continued into adulthood, when Dorothy would also become a well-known novelist.

THE MAKING OF A JOURNALIST

Along with her studies, Willa was very busy with extracurricular activities. Besides her editorial and writing work for *The Hesperian*, Willa was on the staff of other campus literary publications and was the literary editor of her class yearbook. She took part in campus debating clubs and continued to pursue her interest in theater, appearing in some college stage productions.

In her junior year, in 1893, Willa got a job with the *Nebraska State Journal* writing a column of short, fictional sketches about real life. It was her first paying job in journalism and was money Willa needed, as her father was not able to pay for all of her school and living expenses because of financial problems he was having.

Economic times were hard in Nebraska. For several years, there had been very hot, dry summers that resulted in huge crop failures, and by the summer of 1893, the state's economy was very bad. Willa's father had made loans to many farmers who couldn't pay him back. He still owned a large amount of farmland that was heavily mortgaged and was finding it hard to support his family, which now included baby John (Jack), born in 1892.

So Willa became a paid journalist for the last two years of college. After a few months, the paper gave her some feature story assignments in addition to her column work so she could earn more money. It was not easy for her to divide her time between schoolwork, campus publications, and the newspaper. She finally stopped writing stories for *The Hesperian* and concentrated on her work for the *Nebraska State Journal*.

Willa began writing reviews of dramatic and musical plays for the newspaper, and by the second semester of her junior year had become the regular drama critic for the *Journal*. With her love of the arts, Willa wanted to do a good job as an arts critic and took her review writing very seriously. She soon began earning a reputation in the newspaper world as an impressive critic. Willa's reviews were very informative, showing her vast knowledge of drama and literature, as well as a maturity and poise well beyond her years. In an interview later in her life, she spoke about what she thought her job as an arts critic should do: ". . . . reproduce to some extent the atmosphere of the play, to laugh if it was funny, to weep a little if it was sad, to say plainly and frankly if it was bad."

Her reviews conveyed her feelings about the music and gave the readers a feel for the emotions portrayed in the performance. She was also fascinated by the personalities of the artists and wrote long, descriptive paragraphs about the singers. This interest in the lives of artists would one day find its way into her fiction writing.

Willa's last year at the university was taken up with her newspaper work and classes. She was working nearly full time for the newspaper, and her skill as a journalist improved with everything she wrote. She went to classes during the day and spent most evenings at the theater, either at a play or a concert for her work as an arts critic. After the theater, she'd go to the newspaper's office to write her review, often not getting home until very late.

In March of her senior year, Willa was able to get away from both her job and school, to spend a week in Chicago seeing grand opera. It was the high point of her last semester in college. Willa heard a number of operas performed by a world-famous opera company, the New York Metropolitan Opera, and was thrilled and excited by the music and productions. It was the beginning of her lifelong passion for grand opera.

In June of 1895, Willa graduated from the University of Nebraska with a bachelor of arts degree. She was completely worn-out from juggling her newspaper work and schoolwork, but the exhausting time she spent working at the newspaper had been worth it. Willa was not only a college graduate, but also an accomplished journalist.

FIVE

Editor and Critic

After graduation, twenty-one-year-old Willa Cather went home to Red Cloud. She continued writing her reviews and column for the *Journal* newspaper and began another column about books and literature. In August, Cather was offered a position as associate editor of the *Courier*, a Lincoln weekly paper dealing with the arts and society news.

Cather was pleased that she'd made a name for herself as an excellent arts critic, but she wanted to do more than just write columns and reviews and edit art and society news. Cather considered her journalism work her "employment," done to make a living, but her real passion was her fiction writing. That summer and fall, Cather wrote some short stories and sent them to magazines. One story, "On the Divide," was published in the January 1896 issue of the *Overland Monthly*, a national magazine. The story, about a Nebraska farmer, was her first work published in a national magazine.

In the spring of 1896, Cather was offered a full-time editorial job on a new women's magazine, *The Home Monthly*, based in Pittsburgh, Pennsylvania. She left Red Cloud in late June, and by August she was at work on an issue of the magazine. Cather's boss had gone away on a trip soon after she was hired, and Cather was put in charge of the small magazine. For the first issue of the magazine, Cather wrote about half the stories and articles herself because the magazine did not have a large enough budget to allow her to commission stories from well-known writers.

PITTSBURGH LIFE

As Cather settled into her new job and home, she began to meet people and make new friends. Her old friend Dorothy Canfield lived in nearby Columbus, where she was a sophomore at Ohio State University. Canfield visited Pittsburgh, and the two attended plays and other events. Pittsburgh offered lots of entertainment opportunities for a music and

Willa worked for *The Home Monthly* for less than a year as a member of the staff. The magazine cost only 5 cents for one issue.

theater lover like Cather. She went to plays, musicals, opera, symphony, and chamber music concerts, many of them at the beautiful Carnegie Hall Theater, the newest of Pittsburgh's many theaters.

With her love of nature, Cather tried as often as possible to do things in the countryside around the city. She took trips to the mountains and long walks along the riverbanks. Cather felt the rivers of Pittsburgh and the natural beauty of the nearby Ohio countryside helped make up for the rather dirty city, which she found could be depressing on days when it was darkened by river fog and smoke from the coal burned by the city's factories.

MARRIED TO HER WORK

The Home Monthly was a women's magazine aimed at homemakers, with articles about keeping house and raising children. It took only a few months of working on it for Cather to decide that writing about raising

This is a photograph of Pittsburgh, showing the Allegheny River, around the time that Cather lived in the city.

children and keeping house was not interesting to her. Although she didn't like the kind of magazine she was working on, Cather was glad to have a job with a steady income.

Cather may have made a decision during this period in her life to remain single. She had many close male friends, dated occasionally and even received two proposals of marriage (both of which she turned down, saying she was not in love), but she liked being free, and her deepest friendships were with women. In a letter to a friend, Cather wrote about how she enjoyed being her own person with no one but herself to answer to. She thought of herself as an independent woman and enjoyed being able to take care of herself. She was free to do what she wanted with her money, and didn't feel the need to get married for companionship, because she already had lots of friends and a busy life of work and social activities.

From her high school years on, Cather had known she wanted a career and had been determined to attend college. The figures from U.S. census polls taken in the late 1800s showed that college-educated women did not marry as young as other women. Figures also showed at least a quarter of women who graduated from college never married— more than double the proportion of non-college-educated women.

Cather didn't talk to friends about wanting to find a husband and having children. Her interests were always focused on the arts and her writing. Although she loved children and lavished affection on her younger brothers and sisters, she told friends she had no desire to have children of her own.

To Cather, marriage and art did not mix. In a sense, she was married to her art. She believed that good art demanded that an artist lead a life of struggle and isolation. Her writing reflected this belief. In her essays on writers and artists and in her arts columns, Cather wrote about art as "a merciless taskmaster" and said "an artist could not be successful without pouring all his energy and emotion into his art." She understood that there were artists who successfully combined careers with marriage and families, but she knew it was difficult, and seems to have decided she did not want to do this.

VACATIONS AND ILLNESS

In 1897, *The Home Monthly* was sold, and Cather decided to continue writing only a column and occasional story for the magazine. *The Pittsburgh Leader* newspaper offered her a full-time job that she assumed would be as the *Leader*'s drama critic, but she ended up as the telegraph editor—a job normally done by a man. As telegraph editor, Cather edited and developed news cables from foreign correspondents, supplying extra history or background for the news article.

Cather devoted her life to her art. She is shown here hard at work, focused on the thing she loved most, her writing.

The year she worked as telegraph editor was long and hard. She worked at the telegraph desk in the mornings, and in the afternoons and evenings did added work covering special events for the paper. Cather also continued to write columns for the *Nebraska State Journal* and the *Courier* and followed her usual busy social schedule. By summer she was worn-out and returned to Nebraska for two months' vacation. Spending time in Nebraska riding on the prairie and being with her family always renewed Cather.

Back in Pittsburgh in the fall, Cather came down with a serious virus from which it took her months to recover. She was able to contribute only half of her usual work to the newspapers in Pittsburgh and Lincoln and wrote very little fiction. Cather would have recurring health problems like this throughout her life, often due to overwork. Luckily, her life was heading toward changes that would renew her spirit and energy.

A Pittsburgh Pioneer

After just eight months in her new position at *The Pittsburgh Leader,* Cather was included in a feature story in the *Pittsburgh Press* entitled "Pittsburgh's Pioneers in Woman's Progress." The article described in detail twenty-one women involved in nontraditional professions and occupations in Pittsburgh. Along with Cather's editorial job, there were stories on women architects, an embalmer, a physician, a dentist, a real estate agent, a sign painter, and a watchmaker. All were professions that had very few women in them.

From Journalist
to Teacher

By mid-spring of 1899, Cather had finally regained her health and resumed her normal schedule of work, writing, and seeing friends. During this year, Cather met a woman who became a major presence in her life and great inspiration in her work—Isabelle McClung.

A young woman from a socially prominent and wealthy Pittsburgh family, McClung was years younger than Cather and just as passionate about the arts. The two spent a lot of time together, attending concerts and plays, having dinners with friends in the arts, and reading great literature. They both loved nature and took long walks together in parks and along the river. Their friendship grew into a deep love based on mutual respect and affection. McClung gave Cather support and encouragement in her writing, read Cather's work, and offered editorial comments, which Cather valued highly.

By the fall of 1899, Cather was tired of daily journalism. She had been writing for newspapers since her junior year of college and was ready for a change. She quit working for the *Pittsburgh Leader* newspaper in the spring of 1900 and spent the next year working in various jobs, including writing fiction stories for a new weekly periodical and translating letters and documents for a government committee in Washington, D.C.

A DEDICATED TEACHER

In 1901, Cather applied for and landed a job as a Pittsburgh high school teacher and also began writing a column about the arts for the *Pittsburgh Gazette* newspaper. She moved in with Isabelle McClung and her family. The McClungs' house was very different from the small rooming houses Cather had been living in. It was a beautiful, spacious home located in a lovely part of the city.

Isabelle McClung would become one of Cather's closest friends for much of her life.

Cather had her own room on the third floor, as well as a writing study that looked out over the garden and trees. Cather was thrilled with her new living quarters and wrote the first stories she thought were really good there. She began to have more short stories accepted for publication in major magazines, such as the *Saturday Evening Post* and *New England Magazine*.

Teaching was the hardest work Cather had ever done, and the first year of school proved to be exhausting and very demanding. She taught classes in Latin, algebra, English, and composition. When Cather went to Red Cloud for summer vacation, she was so worn-out that she had lost 20 pounds (7.5 kilograms).

As a teacher, Cather was very direct with her students. One of the first things she told her students was how to pronounce her name. It was not pronounced "Kyther" or "Kayther," but rhymed with "Rather." Although she was still in her twenties, her manner was that of an older person. She demanded the attention of her students with a no-nonsense approach.

Cather taught the students in her composition class that the only way to learn to write was to write. She assigned her students writing theme topics each day and taught them "first to observe carefully, then to describe and narrate clearly." Cather assigned a lot of reading. Students were required to memorize poetry and identify different literary devices, such as similes and metaphors. She also made her students look up references to classic mythology. Yet, with all she demanded of her students, Cather's classes were never dull. She often diverged from a lesson to tell them interesting stories about stage or literary personalities she had known.

Her students either loved her or hated her. Cather was blunt in her criticisms of their writing and was hard to please. She graded their writing work rather harshly. She had no patience with students who either couldn't or didn't learn. When she did receive excellent writing, however, she was generous with her praise.

After teaching for nearly a year and a half and saving her money, Cather planned her first trip to Europe: a three-month tour of England and France. Europe was a place she'd wanted to go since she was a child and heard Mrs. Love's stories of France and the immigrants' stories of their homelands. Cather's love of books and plays by European authors and playwrights all contributed to her desire to see Europe.

To bring in some extra money, Cather arranged to send back travel letters to the *Nebraska State Journal* describing her trip. In June of 1902, she and Isabelle McClung sailed to England. Cather was enormously interested in everything she saw and responded with intense emotions she poured into the travel letters she sent back to the *Journal*. She was very taken with the beautiful English countryside, such as this region she described outside the town of Ludlow: "High green hills rise to the north and west, all marked off into tiny pocket

This photograph was taken in 1902, the same year as Cather's trip abroad with Isabelle McClung.

handkerchief fields bordered by green hedgerows and looking like the beds of a large hillside garden."

With her passion for French literature, Cather was especially excited about seeing France. The next six weeks in France were a deeply moving artistic and literary experience for Cather. She and McClung traveled through towns in the French countryside and explored every part of Paris. When she visited the region outside Paris, she wrote that the fields reminded her of the rolling Nebraska prairie. Cather returned home filled with new feelings and emotions from what she'd experienced in Europe.

She resumed teaching and was more determined than ever to publish a book. She had been writing poetry throughout her years in Pittsburgh, so her first book became a collection of poems titled *April Twilights*. It was published in 1903. Some of the poems in the book are dedicated to her family members, such as the poem to her uncle who was killed in the Civil War, and another recalling memories of Cather's time playing beside the Republican River with brothers Roscoe and Douglass.

LIFE-CHANGING EVENTS

In 1903, Cather met two people who became very important in her life: Samuel Sidney (S. S.) McClure and Edith Lewis. Cather met Lewis, a young woman who had just graduated from college, while visiting Lincoln. Lewis was born and raised in Lincoln and wanted to make her career in the world of publishing. She had read Cather's columns as well as one of her short stories, and was an admirer. The two women hit it off

right away, sharing common interests in writing, the arts, and Nebraska. In the years to come, Lewis would become Cather's second-closest friend.

McClure was a publisher who had read some of Cather's stories and wanted to publish them. McClure was a very influential man in publishing who had established a literary syndicate in the United States and was the publisher of *McClure's Magazine*, a major publication that led the muckraking movement with its feature articles exposing illegal activities in big business, government, and in the labor unions. His magazine also published great fiction by renowned writers such as Rudyard Kipling, Stephen Crane, Jack London, Sarah Orne Jewett, Mark Twain, and Arthur Conan Doyle.

McClure published a collection of Cather's stories in 1905. Given the title *The Troll Garden*, the collection contained seven of her stories, all of which dealt with art and artists. The reviewers saw promise in Cather's writing, and the book sold a moderate number of copies.

After the book came out and the 1905 school year ended, Cather and McClung traveled west. They spent a week with Cather's brother Douglass in Cheyenne, Wyoming, and a week camping in the Black Hills, South Dakota, with her brother Roscoe. Cather was growing to love the western part of the country more and more.

In the early spring of 1906, McClure asked Cather to join his staff in New York as an editor. She accepted and resigned her teaching job. In Pittsburgh, Cather had had many new experiences and met lots of interesting people in the arts, adding more memories to her writer's brain, which was already crowded with images and stories from Virginia, Red Cloud, and Lincoln. Now Cather got ready for life in another new place.

The Muckrakers

In the late 1800s and early 1900s, the rise of industry brought growth and change to the United States. It also brought corruption. Some American writers who wrote both fiction and nonfiction used their work to expose corruption in business and politics. They were called the muckrakers, a term first used by President Theodore Roosevelt in 1906. Two notable muckrakers were Ray Stannard Baker and Ida Tarbell. Both authors wrote important investigative articles in *McClure's Magazine*. Baker exposed corruption in the United Mine Workers of America Union, and Tarbell wrote an investigative series on J. D. Rockefeller's Standard Oil Company.

The commencement exercises will be held May 31 to June 7th. The baccalaureate sermon will be preached by Charles Edward Locke, D. D., of Brooklyn, N. Y., and the commencement address will be delivered by Bishop John H. Vincent, D. D., LL. D., of Indianapolis.

———

The following letter has been sent by Miss Cather to her reporting class in 307 and because we think every one would like to hear from her, especially those who have known her in any time of their course we desire, with the permission of the class we publish it.

We are truly sorry to hear that Miss Cather will not return, and we count it the saddest event of our school year. We, however, would rather grieve at her departure than not to have known her at all, for we feel that we have gained by being near her. We are proud of her success, and as friends we wish her the best of luck, much happiiness, the fulfillment of her desires and a splendid future:

June 2, 1906.

To My Reporting Class:

Dear Boys and Girls:—Now that I find that I shall not return to the High School next fall, I have a word to say to you. A number of my pupils in various classes, and especially in my Reporting Class, asked me, when I came away, whether I should be with you next year. At that time I fully expected to be. The changes in my plans which will prevent my doing so have been sudden an unforeseen. I should hate to have you think that I had not answered you squarely when you were good enough to ask whether I should return, or to have you think that I put you off with an excuse.

I had made many plans for your Senior work next year and had hoped that we should enjoy that work together. I must now leave you to enjoy it alone. One always has to choose between good things, it seems. So I turn to a work I love, with very real regret that I must leave behind, for the time, at least, a work I had come to love almost as well. But I much more regret having to take leave of so many students whom I feel are good friends of mine. As long as I stay in New York I shall always be glad to see any of my students when they come to the city.

I wish you every success in your coming examinations and in your senior work next year.

Faithfully always,

WILLA S. CATHER.

———

Editing a magazine is a nice thing. If we publish jokes, people say we are rattle-brained. If we don't, we are fossils. If we publish original matter they say we don' t give them enough selections. If we give them selections they say we are too lazy to write. If we don't go to church we are heathens. If we go we are hypocrites. If we remain in the office, we ought to go out and hustle. If we go out, then we are not tending to business. If we wear old clothes they laugh at us. If we wear good clothes they say we have a pull. Now, what are we to do? Just as likely as not some one will say we stole this from an exchange. So we did.

———

What appropriate gift is Ethel going to give Bob on class night?

———

Freddie is the queen of May.

———

Where did Grace G. go on Decoration Day?

———

Lefty finds that even the dignified Romans stooped so low as to say "23."

This is Cather's good-bye note to her students, which appeared in a school publication.

SEVEN

The World of Publishing

When Cather arrived in New York City to work on the magazine, McClure had just bought out his partners, and most of his former editorial associates and staff were gone. A new staff was hired, including Cather's friend Edith Lewis, who was employed as a proofreader. They got to work putting out the magazine. McClure proved to be a difficult man to work for. He was continually cutting and revising copy, and the staff had trouble trying to finish articles and meet deadlines. Although McClure was a troublesome boss, Cather admired him and felt she was learning a great deal about the publishing business from him.

For Cather, *McClure's Magazine* was as unusual a magazine to work for as *Home Monthly* had been. She had little interest in the muckraking journalism in the publication just as she had no interest in *Home Monthly*'s homemaking articles. What she did love about *McClure's* was the literature it published. She was excited about working with important writers.

Cather moved into a studio apartment on Washington Square in a part of New York City known as Greenwich Village. She lived in the same building as Edith Lewis, and the magazine office was about twenty blocks away. Greenwich Village was a pleasant place to live, and Washington Square was especially nice. The north side was lined by attractive brick

Cather's first apartment was on this street on the south side of Washington Square. Many artists and writers had studios in the area at the time.

houses, and across the square, larger apartment buildings were occupied by writers and artists.

Cather had visited New York City a number of times during her years in Pittsburgh. She found living there was both challenging and exciting. The city was big, noisy, and dirty. It was stimulating and always interesting. Cather loved the arts and social life, fine restaurants, and rich cultural life.

BOSTON AND BEYOND

While at *McClure's*, Cather was asked to rewrite and finish researching a manuscript on the life of Mary Baker Eddy, the founder of the Christian Science religion. To do the research, Cather went to Boston, where she lived for most of 1907 and part of 1908. She was excited about seeing

New York in 1906

New York in 1906 was a bustling city that was growing every day. Ellis Island off the waterfront of lower Manhattan was a major processing station for people entering the United States, and twelve million immigrants came through the island from 1892 to 1954. New York had a rich ethnic mix of people and was home to the garment, publishing, and financial industries, and was a growing center for the arts. Its famous landmarks at the time included the Statue of Liberty, Central Park, the Bronx Zoo, the Brooklyn Bridge, the Metropolitan Museum of Art, and the Metropolitan Opera House.

Boston for the first time and toured many of the city's landmarks. While staying in the Boston area, Cather also took time to travel to other parts of New England, including the White Mountains of New Hampshire, a place she would return to many times in her life.

During her time in Boston, Cather made an important new friend. Through a mutual acquaintance, Cather met an author named Sarah Orne Jewett. Cather had read Jewett's books and liked them very much, especially *The Country of the Pointed Firs*. Jewett was much older than Cather and was the first important woman writer Cather knew well. The two began what became a deep friendship.

Cather was promoted to managing editor at *McClure's*. Her work there was going well, but her own fiction writing had taken a backseat to the magazine. She published four stories in 1907, but these had been written before leaving Pittsburgh. In 1908, she wrote just one story. Cather was frustrated at not having the time and energy to work on more fiction.

In 1908, Cather got an apartment with Edith Lewis a few blocks away from their old apartment house on Washington Square. Lewis now had her own career as a magazine editor and an advertising writer, and the two had developed a close friendship. They were good roommates and lived together very happily.

REFLECTION AND DECISIONS

The only story Cather published in 1908 was in *McClure's Magazine*. It was called "On the Gull's Road," and Cather had many doubts about its quality. She sent a copy to Sarah Orne Jewett and asked for her opinion.

Jewett wrote Cather a long letter offering some advice.

She told Cather that her writing was being hindered by the work she was doing for the magazine. She thought it was impossible for Cather to be a magazine editor and at the same time work on her writing so that her writing talent would mature properly. She should have quiet places in which to write so she could concentrate more on her work. Jewett went on to tell her that she needed to find a private place inside herself to write from, using memories and images of her own.

"I want you to be surer of your backgrounds, you have your Nebraska life, a child's Virginia. . . . You must write to the human heart. . . . You can write about life, but never life itself. . . . You need to have time to yourself and time to read and add to your recognitions."

Jewett's letter touched Cather deeply. Cather responded with an eight-page reply in which she deeply analyzed herself and her prospects, ambitions, and talents. Cather admitted that she often thought of trying to get three or four months a year of free time

Edith Lewis would remain close friends with Cather for the rest of her life.

to write, but it was difficult to hand the details of the magazine over to anyone else. Jewett's warnings and advice made Cather decide to make changes in her life. She'd take some time off from the magazine as soon as possible and work solely on her fiction.

Sarah Orne Jewett died unexpectedly less than a year later, and Cather was overcome with grief when she heard the news. Jewett had become Cather's mentor and an extremely important literary influence.

In the summer of 1911, Cather was preparing to take a six-month leave from the magazine when she learned that *McClure's* was changing ownership. S. S. McClure had lost control of the company and the magazine during a financial reorganization of the business. Cather was distressed for McClure, but didn't quit her job at the magazine. She insisted on taking her leave and traveled with Isabelle McClung to a rented house in upstate New York for three months of quiet and writing.

The necklace that Cather wore in this photograph was said to be a gift from Sarah Orne Jewett. Jewett's death deeply saddened Cather.

EIGHT

A Writer Finds Her Voice

Cather finished a short novel titled *Alexander's Masquerade* that was scheduled to appear in three parts in *McClure's* starting in February of 1912. She sent the completed manuscript to *McClure's* and also to her editor friend Ferris Greenslet at Houghton Mifflin Company in Boston. Greenslet liked it and told Cather that Houghton Mifflin would publish it as a book after it ran in the magazine.

Fired up with creative energy, Cather worked on two more stories, "The Bohemian Girl" and "Alexandra." Each made use of her memories of the immigrant families and the Nebraska prairie. Cather worked on the stories through the fall and winter and finished them by February, when *Alexander's Masquerade* began to run in *McClure's*. Deciding to take a break from writing, Cather began making preparations for a trip to visit her brother Douglass, who then lived in Winslow, Arizona. In April,

Houghton Mifflin published *Alexander's Masquerade* under a new title, *Alexander's Bridge*.

After it was published, Cather decided she wasn't happy with her first novel. She thought she had made a mistake by not writing about an experience she felt completely comfortable with. *Alexander's Bridge* follows the story of a man who builds bridges and the conflicts he faces in his personal and work life. Her novel didn't come from deep inside. She said later in an interview, "I had been trying to sing a song that did not lie in my own voice."

A SOUTHWESTERN TURNING POINT

The trip to see Douglass was Willa's first visit to that part of the Southwest. As her train rolled through New Mexico and Arizona, Cather was stunned by the beauty of the country. She was especially taken with the incredible colors of the mountains. Cather wrote a friend that she thought it was the most beautiful country she had seen anywhere, even more brilliant than the coast of France.

Douglass took her on many day trips into the areas surrounding Winslow and to other parts of Arizona, including the Grand Canyon. They hiked a good deal, as they had in their childhood when they roamed the Divide.

During one outing, Willa and Douglass visited some ruins of ancient cliff dwellings in Walnut Canyon, Arizona. Cather was fascinated by the cliff dwellings and decided that someday she would have to go back to the Southwest to see more. Years later, she used a description of them in one of her books, *The Song of the Lark*: "There a stratum of rock . . . [that] had

Willa and Douglass Cather take a break from exploring the ruins of cliff dwellings in Walnut Canyon, Arizona.

Cliff Dwellings

Ancient people sometimes made their homes in natural caves in cliffs or under cliff overhangs. The remains of their cliff homes have been found in many areas of the world, but the American Southwest has the largest concentration of them. The cliff dwellings date from about A.D. 900 to about 1450. The Ancestral Puebloan people are among the cultures that built the cliff dwellings. Made of stone or mud blocks, the structures were built in the shallow caves and recesses of the canyon sides, and served as natural shelters from the weather. Most of them had to be entered either by removable ladders or by hand- and footholds cut into the cliffs.

been hollowed out. . . . In this hollow . . . the Ancient People had built their houses of yellowish stone and mortar. . . . The houses stood along in a row, like the buildings in a city block. . . ."

Full of creative energy, Cather traveled from Arizona to Red Cloud. The trip was a turning point in her life. Visiting the Southwest, seeing the beautiful country and the ruins of the cliff dwellings, and learning about the ancient cultures, made her look at Nebraska and its people and culture in a new way. She had a fresh appreciation for the quiet beauty of the prairie and its wide-open spaces and for the history of the people who lived there. As she visited old neighbors in the farm country on the Divide and watched the wheat farmers working in the fields, Cather thought about how their grandparents conquered the land through their hard work. She remembered the old women talking of the customs they brought with them from their home countries.

Modern inventions now made their work easier and more productive, and they could afford to buy more material things instead of

From Handmade to Machine Made

From 1870 to 1900, the United States became the world's foremost industrial nation. Industrialization—the change from making goods by hand to manufacturing goods with machines—transformed commerce, the environment, the workplace, the home, and everyday life. Manufactured goods seem to make people's lives easier, and soon everyone wanted these "modern" goods, which found their way into even the poorest homes.

making everything themselves. Life seemed easier and better, but Cather wondered if something was being lost—the pioneer spirit of hard work and pride in the land.

Cather left Red Cloud wanting to write a novel about all her experience there—the Nebraska prairie, the immigrants, the spirit of the pioneer. The two stories she'd completed before her trip to the Southwest, "The Bohemian Girl" and "Alexandra," were based on Nebraska memories, and after arriving back in New York, she wrote "The White Mulberry Tree." Each story conveyed some of the ideas about Nebraska and the immigrants that she wanted to write about, but none of them was coming together into an idea for a novel.

Then Cather took "Alexandra" and read it alongside "The White Mulberry Tree" and a light went off inside her head as she realized the two stories went together. She later told friends that this was a life-changing moment for her, and that she could only describe this coming together of the two elements as a sudden inner explosion and enlightenment. Cather had experienced it before only when she'd written a poem. She hoped now that she would always have a similar experience when creating a novel. The explosion seemed to bring with it the shape of the novel, which was not from being plotted out, but filtered through her blood after months of living with an idea until the material had designed itself.

From that point on, Cather became a strong believer in organic form—letting the material dictate the organization and structure of the writing. Ten years later, in a new preface she wrote for *Alexander's Bridge*, Cather described this writing process: "When a writer begins to work with his own material . . . he has less and less power of choice about the molding of it. It seems to be there of itself, already molded."

Over the next few months, eager to concentrate on writing her new novel, Cather made changes to her life. She stopped doing editorial work at the magazine and agreed only to write articles or short stories. Cather and Edith Lewis also moved to a bigger, better apartment in Greenwich Village that had a nice study where she could write. Cather loved the new apartment. It had seven large rooms with high ceilings and big windows to let in lots of sunlight, and was close to a library that she used often.

By the start of 1913, she'd finished her Nebraska novel, titled *O Pioneers!* (the title borrowed from the title of a Walt Whitman poem). Cather sent it to Houghton Mifflin, which agreed to publish it at the end of June. Cather started writing a series of articles on the arts, and began working with S. S. McClure on his autobiography, which she had agreed to write for him. McClure had been a difficult man to work for, but Cather had learned a great deal from him. She was grateful for the years she worked at the magazine, which allowed her to travel to interesting places and meet many people in the publishing and arts worlds.

The next months were hectic but fulfilling. Cather was very happy being able to work on her novels or short fiction in the mornings for about two and a half to three hours every day. Some days, Cather worked for a longer period but she never forced herself into working because she felt she wouldn't gain anything by it. Cather wrote fiction only because she loved it. In one interview she said, "I write . . . because it interests me more than any other activity I've ever found. I like riding, going to operas and concerts, travel in the West, but on the whole writing interests me more than anything else."

In April of 1914, Cather was working on an arts article for *McClure's* called "Three American Singers" and interviewed a well-known opera singer named Olive Fremstad. Cather had seen Fremstad perform and had been very impressed by her. After the interview, Cather thought how much Fremstad reminded her of the strong immigrant farm women of Nebraska and also of herself as an artist. Both women had worked hard to make their careers in the arts. Cather decided to use Fremstad as a character in a book.

When *O Pioneers!* was published in June of 1913, Cather was delighted that her family and friends were enthusiastic about the book. She was pleased at the good reviews she got in newspapers and magazines, especially the ones from the prairie states, and saved them all. The reviewers recognized Cather as a new voice in American literature and her Nebraska plains setting as a new locale for American fiction.

O Pioneers!

Cather's novel, set on the prairie, is the story of the daughter of Swedish immigrant farmers who is forced to assume responsibility for the farm and family after her father's death in nineteenth-century Nebraska. Her devotion to the land sustains her against the hardships and suffering of prairie life. It is Cather's story of the early struggles of the Swedish and Bohemian settlers she knew in Nebraska in which she pays tribute to their lives.

In an interview she gave at the time, Cather said, "The reviews have concerned themselves a good deal more with the subject matter of the story than with my way of telling it, and I am glad of that. I care a lot more about the country and the people than I care about my own way of writing. . . ."

The autobiography of S. S. McClure was published as a book in the spring of 1914 under the title *My Autobiography*. Only McClure's name was listed as the author—Cather was the "behind the scenes" writer, something she did not mind because of all McClure had done for her, and because she'd enjoyed working with him on the book. She was pleased that the autobiography received praise for its excellent writing.

NINE

New Inspirations

Cather began working on her next book, using Olive Fremstad's life story. It was a book about an immigrant girl who becomes a famous opera star. Cather felt that Fremstad's journey to becoming an opera singer was close to Cather's own journey to becoming a fiction writer. Both had worked hard as children to cultivate their natural gifts. Each had worked and saved to pay for their education, and it had taken both women a long time to finally have the career each wanted. As Cather wrote, the book became not only the story of an opera singer, but of Cather herself.

Cather worked on the book until February of 1915, when she was once again hospitalized for a serious illness. She spent the next few months recuperating in Pittsburgh and at her parents' home in Red Cloud. While in Nebraska, in September, Cather listened to news reports about World War I, which had started the year before in Europe. She was upset by the terrible reports of death and devastation in many countries.

Cather finished her opera novel, titled *The Song of the Lark*, and sent it to Houghton Mifflin in March of 1915. She then finished writing the last of the arts articles she was doing for *McClure's*, and except for two stories the magazine later published, Cather was done with the publication. She had worked for more than six years at *McClure's*, sharing her fiction writing with her editorial work. She was free now to concentrate on her fiction, but the war taking place in Europe was all she could think about.

INSPIRATION FROM ANCIENT PEOPLE

Too disturbed by the war to concentrate on writing, Cather planned a trip with Edith Lewis back out to the Southwest to see more of the cliff dwellings. In the summer of 1915, they traveled to Colorado and Mesa

World War I

Called "the Great War," World War I began in 1914 and involved many countries of the world. Fought between the Central Powers (Germany, Austria-Hungary, Bulgaria, and Turkey) and the Allied countries (Great Britain, France, Italy, Japan, Portugal, Russia, and the United States) and many other countries besides, the war brought great destruction to many European countries. About eight million soldiers died in the war. The war ended in 1918 when the Allies defeated the Central Powers.

Verde National Park, where there is the largest collection of cliff dwellings in the United States. They stopped in Mancos, Colorado, near Mesa Verde National Park, to visit the brother of Richard Wetherill, one of the two cowboys who in 1888 discovered the famous ruin called Cliff Palace, one of the many cliff dwellings at Mesa Verde. Cather heard the exciting story of how Wetherill found the structures, and she would later use some of this story in a novel.

Cather and Lewis spent a week touring the Mesa Verde cliff dwellings with a guide. They spent an entire day exploring the Cliff Palace, which

The title for *The Song of the Lark* was taken from a Jules Breton painting Willa had seen in the Chicago Art Institute that was of a peasant girl stopping on her way to work to listen to a skylark bird.

Cather stands among the ruins at Mesa Verde during a visit to the Southwest in 1915.

Cowboy Discovery

Richard Wetherill found the cliff dwellings with another cowboy as they were chasing stray cattle. Crossing the Mancos River on horses, they rode up a deep canyon, following it until they reached its center. Leaving their horses, they climbed up another wide canyon. After a long period of hard climbing, Richard Wetherill happened to look up at the great cliffs above him, and had his first glimpse of the cliff dwellings.

had a tower and more than 151 rooms. Cather was fascinated by these structures and by the history of the ancient Ancestral Puebloan people who had built them. The guide provided the history of the culture while Cather and Lewis looked through the windows and climbed around the ruins.

From Mesa Verde, Cather and Lewis went to Taos, New Mexico, to see the desert in that region. The entire trip had a transforming effect on the writer. Cather felt intensely alive in this western area, and she went back to the East with the same feelings of renewal and creativity she had gotten after exploring the Southwest with her brother three years before.

Fresh with creative inspiration, Cather went to Red Cloud. She was still in Red Cloud when *The Song of the Lark* was published in October. Most reviewers of the novel were enthusiastic. Cather was pleased to hear from Olive Fremstad that she loved the book. This was another novel close to her heart, and Cather expressed many of her feelings about her writing life through the character of the opera singer in the book: "Your work becomes your personal life. You are not much good until it does. . . . It takes you up and uses you, and spits you out, and that is your life. Not much else can happen to you."

Stories From the Heart

In late fall of 1915, Isabelle McClung told Cather she was going to marry a concert violinist named Jan Hambourg. Cather wrote to a friend, expressing sadness that McClung's marriage would bring a big change to their relationship. The two women had been best friends for years. Though they would remain close, Cather knew their relationship would be different with McClung sharing her life with a husband.

BOOKS ABOUT NEBRASKA AND WAR

After attending Isabelle and Jan Hambourg's wedding in April of 1916, Cather made another trip to the Southwest. She visited Douglass in Colorado, then went on to Taos, New Mexico, and finally to see her brother Ross and his family in Lander, Wyoming. Cather had a great time with Ross's family fishing, horseback riding, and hiking in the mountains. Her Southwest trip again recharged her creative energy. Cather went to Red Cloud intending to write. She had written a story about an opera singer during a brief stop in Denver and she was eager to write another. She also planned to begin a novel set in the Southwest, to be called *The Blue Mesa*.

While in Red Cloud, Cather visited her old friend Anna Sadilek, who was now married to a Czech farmer named John Pavelka. When she was younger, Anna had returned quietly to Webster County. At that time, she was an unwed mother who had been deserted by a man who worked for the railroad. Anna had given birth to a daughter, who she raised herself until she met and married Pavelka.

Cather's trip to the Pavelka farm and her talks with Anna started her thinking about a story that would involve Anna and her life. Troubled by what she saw as a loss of spiritual values that accompanied the growth of materialism and technology, Cather wanted to tell another story about the pioneer spirit and the values that accompanied it. She put aside *The Blue Mesa* and began to work on her new idea.

Cather wrote all winter, and by spring was halfway through the first draft of the new book, now titled *My Ántonia*. In June of 1917, she went to the University of Nebraska to receive an honorary degree (the first honorary degree the school had awarded to a woman), and in the late summer, she went to see the Hambourgs at their summer house in Jaffrey, New Hampshire.

This was Cather's first time in this region of New Hampshire, and she loved the natural beauty and serenity of the countryside. She decided to stay and finish *My Ántonia*. Two friends from Pittsburgh who had rented a home in Jaffrey set up a writing studio for Cather in a tent in their meadow. She loved the "tent studio." In the mornings after breakfast she wrote in her tent for two or three hours, and in the afternoons, she took long walks through the countryside and up the mountain trails. Cather came back to work in Jaffrey for many years.

Cather finished *My Ántonia* in June of 1918 and traveled to Red Cloud. While there, Cather visited her Aunt Frances Cather (Aunt Franc) and read the letters her cousin Grosvenor wrote to his mother before he was killed in a battle in France on May 28, 1918. He was the first Nebraska officer to die in battle during World War I and had received a citation for bravery just before he was killed.

Cather had known Grosvenor since they were both children in Nebraska, but they had drifted apart and seldom saw each other after she went to college. Reading his letters brought back memories of their childhood and an idea for a book.

My Ántonia was published in late September of 1918. The reviewers were nearly unanimous in their praise, recognizing the novel as a significant contribution to American literature. Cather was very happy with the novel and said at the time that it was "the best thing I've ever done. . . . I feel I've made a contribution to American letters in that book."

She used many of her childhood memories of Nebraska in the story, such as the train ride from Virginia to Nebraska when she was nine years old and her first glimpses of the barren prairies and her grandfather's farm. Cather's descriptions of the western prairie are alive with feeling: "The road ran about like a wild thing. . . . And all along it, wherever it looped or ran, the sunflowers grew. . . . They made a gold ribbon across the prairie."

A STORY FROM THE FAMILY

Back in New York in the fall, Cather started writing a book inspired by her cousin's letters. This story used a different writing style than her previous books had. Cather wanted to explore the inner thinking and consciousness of her characters, focusing on their spiritual and cultural crises and struggles to find meaning in their lives. She decided to tell the story using a third-person narrator who continually slips into the main character's consciousness, giving the reader a view of the world through the main character's perceptions.

Her story would follow the principal character from his life as a farmer to the army and France where he would meet a fellow officer

My Ántonia

This book is Cather's best-known work. Since its publication, the novel has been considered a literary classic and is often used in literature courses in schools. Told through a narrator, the story recounts the history of Ántonia Shimerda (drawn from the real Anna Sadilek Pavelka), the daughter of Bohemian immigrants who settled on the Nebraska frontier. It tells Ántonia's story as she returns to Black Hawk (Red Cloud), Nebraska, to make a new start after eloping with a railway conductor following the tragic death of her father. *My Ántonia* honors the immigrant settlers of the American plains and uses the character of the immigrant Ántonia, with her strength and passion, as a symbol of the pioneer West. Ántonia was Cather's alternative to the typical Western symbol of a cowboy, mountain man, or gunfighter.

who had been a concert violinist before enlisting and being introduced to a new world. The model for the concert violinist was based on a real-life concert violinist named David Hochstein, whom Cather had once interviewed for an article.

People in New York City take to the streets to celebrate the end of World War I.

She found some writing easy, especially the beginning sections that took place in Nebraska, but the parts about the war and fighting in France were more difficult. Cather turned to her old friend Dorothy Canfield for help with the parts about France and French culture. She also sought out soldiers in New York who had returned from the war, especially anyone from Nebraska, to speak to them about their experiences. She later traveled to France and toured battlegrounds, making notes for her book.

The end of World War I came in November of 1918, and Cather joined the rest of the country in celebrating. She wrote to her Aunt Franc, telling her how she mourned that her cousin had not lived to see the glorious day of victory.

PUBLISHER PROBLEMS

While working on the book, Cather changed publishers. She was unhappy with Houghton Mifflin because of money matters and the lack of marketing being done on her books, and moved to Alfred A. Knopf. In 1920 Cather put together a collection of short stories about artists and musicians called *Youth and the Bright Medusa* and Knopf published it. They did a great job with the book, giving it a beautiful design and handsome graphics. The first printing sold out quickly with the help of the company's excellent advertising.

A Literary Heritage

Cather worked on her war novel until the early spring of 1921. Then she went to see the Hambourgs in Toronto, Canada, in order to spend some time with them before they moved to France. Cather wanted to finish her novel while in Toronto, but at first writing proved to be impossible because she was bombarded with invitations to parties and requests for speeches and interviews.

After the publication and success of *O Pioneers!*, Cather started receiving many requests to give interviews, to deliver speeches, and to attend events. At first she enjoyed her newfound celebrity status and accepted the requests. But as the demands on her time grew and she found less time to write, the invitations became less and less appealing. Discovering this same overwhelming onslaught of requests in Canada upset her very much. She would grow to hate and resent the "celebrity" element of her career.

Cather finished her novel by the end of August. After sending it to her publisher, Knopf, she began work on a book about Lyra Garber, the wife of Silas Garber, a former governor of Nebraska. Lyra had been the leading lady of Red Cloud when Cather was growing up. She'd read about Lyra's death and wanted to write about her. Cather hoped to capture the essence of Lyra's personality. She wrote of a talented woman who was trapped in the social conventions and economic restrictions of marriage but who would defy expectations and make deep, personal changes through inner exploration and renewed spirituality. She titled it *The Lost Lady*.

With the writing of her war novel and *The Lost Lady*, Cather's work began to move toward a more intense exploration of society and the nature of faith, religion, and spirituality. Through the years, Cather had grown more distressed about what she felt was modern society's reliance on materialism and mechanization and the loss of spirituality in the world. Also disturbed by the war and its destruction, Cather herself was feeling the need for more spirituality in her life.

She'd grown up a Baptist in Red Cloud, and her family always attended church, but in college she left the church when she went through a period of skepticism about God. She hadn't thought much about religion and

Cather enjoys a quiet moment by the water on Grand Manan Island.

faith in the years after college. Now older and more concerned about the loss of the old values in society, she began to see that it was tied to a loss of spirituality. In 1921, she was close to turning fifty years old. She was reflecting more and more on the state of the world. Cather's state of mind was reflected in her writing.

Cather wasn't alone in her worry over the state of American values. In the 1920s, other authors, such as T. S. Eliot, Ezra Pound, Edna St. Vincent Millay, Sinclair Lewis, F. Scott Fitzgerald, and Ernest Hemingway, were troubled by the growing mechanization and mass-produced quality of American society. Feeling alienated from the accepted values of American culture, these writers also used their books to confront these issues.

Cather was in and out of hospitals with different ailments over the next few months. When her health returned, she went to Montreal, Canada, to the Grand Manan Island in the Bay of Fundy, a place she had always wanted to visit. She was immediately charmed by the beauty and isolation of the island and rented a quiet cottage in a small resort area called Whale Cove. The quiet natural setting inspired her to work, and she did a lot of writing there.

Cather's war novel, now titled *One of Ours,* was published on September 8, 1922. The reviews of this book were mixed. Some important reviewers were very hostile to the book, comparing it unfavorably to other war books that had come out at the same time. *One of Ours* was criticized as being too feminine. Reviewers particularly did not like Cather's war scenes, which they felt they were not authentic.

Many others in the literary world praised the way Cather explored her main characters' inner lives and emotions. The favorable reviews actually outnumbered the unfavorable ones by about two to one. Cather received a large amount of enthusiastic fan mail, many from ex-soldiers, and *One of Ours* not only became a best-seller, but earned her the Pulitzer Prize for fiction in 1923.

Even with the praise and letters, Cather was deeply wounded by the negative reviews. She had lived with the book's story inside her for three years as she worked on it, and it was the only one she had written up to that point whose main character was based on a family member. She became even more protective of both her work and her privacy. In 1925, she told an interviewer, "I like best of my books the one that all the high-brow critics knock. In my opinion, *One of Ours* has more of value in it than any one of the others."

WRITING ABOUT INNER LIVES

At the end of November 1922, Cather went home to Red Cloud to attend her parents' fiftieth wedding anniversary celebration. All of Cather's brothers and sisters came for the occasion, and she felt happy at home surrounded by family. She had five nieces and nephews now growing up in Red Cloud, and Cather was very interested in spending time with them and finding out how they were doing. The children were always excited when they heard that Aunt Willie was coming. Cather's niece Helen (brother James's daughter) remembered as an adult that her fondest childhood memories were helping Aunt Willie unpack her trunk, which contained elegant city clothes for the afternoon and evening—heavy silk crepe skirts and chiffon and crepe de chine blouses and dresses. Cather had grown into a woman who liked to dress up, and she wore the same clothes in Red Cloud that she did in New York City.

Along with the golden wedding anniversary, another important event took place in Red Cloud during that stay. Continuing her search for a spiritual renewal, Cather finally found what she wanted in the Episcopal Church. Willa, along with her parents, joined the church and remained loyal members of the Red Cloud congregation. When her father died, Cather gave the church a stained-glass window in his memory.

In 1923, *A Lost Lady* was published. Cather's book expressed her profoundly modern, feminist views through her portrayal of a strong, vital woman who refuses to be beaten by adversity. The book dealt with Cather's continuing frustration with modern society and its sense of spiritual decay. Cather hoped her book had captured the essence of the real Lyra Garber.

In an interview, Cather said that the problem in writing *A Lost Lady* was to capture Lyra, not like a typical heroine in fiction, but as she really

was: "I didn't try to make a character study, but a portrait like a thin miniature painted on ivory . . .[to] get her just as I remembered her and produce the effect she had on me and the many others who knew her."

A Lost Lady received praise from both reviewers and ordinary readers, and Warner Brothers made a movie from it in 1925.

Willa Cather enjoyed the opportunity to spend time with her family at her parents' wedding anniversary celebration. She is photographed here with some of her nieces.

Cather wasn't happy about that because she didn't like movies—they were another of the modern inventions she felt were ruining society. Later, she wrote a provision in her will that prohibited any future dramatizations of her books in any form.

STORIES FROM THE SOUTHWEST

In 1923, Cather plunged into the writing of her next novel, *The Professor's House*. The next two years were productive. Along with finishing *The Professor's House*, Cather put together an edition of Sarah Orne Jewett's best stories for Houghton Mifflin. She earned her second honorary degree, from the University of Michigan in Ann Arbor, and published her first magazine story in five years, "Uncle Valentine," which is considered to be one of her best pieces of short fiction.

Cather traveled to the Southwest again in 1925. While staying at a hotel in Santa Fe, she came across a rare book that gave her information about the lives and work of the missionary priests in the Southwest. On one of her early trips to the West, Cather heard some interesting stories about a pioneering French priest in the Southwest and had wanted to learn more about him.

Some sources say that she bought this fur coat with the money she earned from *The Professor's House*.

Finding the book about missionary priests instantly sparked the plot for a novel about a French priest's life in the Southwest. She started working on the novel, giving it the title *Death Comes for the Archbishop*.

"What I write," she said years later in an interview, "results from a personal explosional experience. All of a sudden, the idea for a story is in my head. It is in the ink bottle when I start to write. But I don't start until the idea has found its own pattern. . . ."

The Professor's House was published in September of 1925. It is a psychological study. The story is about a history professor in his fifties who struggles with his disillusionment with his materialistic wife and daughters, with changing university education, and with modern life in general. This main story is wrapped around another story that is titled *Tom Outland's Story*. It is the tale of a western adventurer's discovery of the ruins of cliff dwellings in the Southwest, based on Richard Wetherill's discovery of the ruins in Mesa Verde, Colorado. The book again reflected Cather's spiritual searching and troubled thinking at the time she wrote it.

During the next year, Cather continued to work on *Death Comes for the Archbishop*. Cather's writing entered a third stage with this novel. Her next books were based on historical themes and explored not only her characters' relationship with the land, but also the tension between their Old World values and life in a new land. They were a critical view of the present that reflected what Cather had come to feel as she grew older.

In October of 1926, Cather published a short novel titled *My Mortal Enemy*. It was a gloomy picture of a marriage and one of her most dramatic novels. About a year later, *Death Comes for the Archbishop* was published. Not only was the book a great critical triumph but readers also loved it. The novel became a best-seller and was her greatest financial success. Many critics considered this book to be the strongest example of a work reflecting Cather's moral and spiritual concerns.

The success of her book brought a joyful moment to Cather during a difficult period. Cather and Lewis had been forced to move from the apartment they'd lived in for fifteen years because the building was going to be torn down, and in the spring of 1928, Cather's father died from a heart attack. She was overcome with grief. Her brother Douglass now lived in California and took their mother there. Cather remained alone in Red Cloud for more than a month, wanting to stay near memories of her father.

The emotional drain took its toll, and Cather got very sick after returning to New York City. When Cather was well enough, she and Lewis left for Grand Manan Island so Cather could recuperate further. On the way there, they took a side trip to visit Quebec, a city Cather hadn't seen before. The stopover in Quebec turned out to be the beginning of a new book.

Death Comes for the Archbishop

One of Cather's best-known novels, this book explores the vanished past of the American Southwest, where nature and Christianity are opposed to modern urban life and society. In the novel, Cather traces the friendship and adventures of a Roman Catholic bishop and a priest as they organize a new Roman Catholic district in New Mexico. It is based on the real lives of Bishop Jean Baptiste Lamy and Father Joseph Machebeuf, two French missionaries who had been boyhood friends and were both living in New Mexico just after the Mexican War.

TWELVE

Final Chapters

Quebec reminded Cather of the old French towns she'd seen years before. She knew right away she wanted to make Quebec the subject of a new novel. Cather and Lewis went on to Grand Manan, where Cather saw the new summer cottage she had ordered built during the past year. It was primitive: no indoor plumbing, no telephone, and no electricity, but Cather loved it. It was the first and only house she would ever own. To have the beauty and peace of the seashore and forests, she'd give up a few conveniences.

BAD NEWS AND TOUGH TIMES

After two restful months in her new cottage, Cather returned to New York, ready to begin work on her Quebec novel, entitled *Shadows on the*

Rock. She was interrupted by news that her mother, who was still staying with Douglass in California, had a stroke that left her paralyzed on one side and almost unable to speak. Cather went to help her brother look after their mother. It was hard for her to see her mother so ill.

Her mother improved a little, and Cather had to leave California a few months later to go to Yale University to receive another honorary doctorate degree. She returned to Grand Manan to work on *Shadows on the Rock*. Over the next two years, Cather spent most of her time working on the novel and visiting her mother, who was becoming weaker and sicker. Cather found it difficult to watch her mother suffering without being able to help her.

Along with the death and illness of her parents, Cather was deeply concerned about how the sad state of the nation's economy affected the people she knew. The country had entered a terrible economic time in the late 1920s called the Great Depression. Many of Cather's old farm friends in Nebraska and friends and relatives in other states were in desperate need. Cather was doing well from money earned from her books.

While in Quebec, Cather visited all the historic spots in the city, and read the history of Canada in her hotel's library.

She began helping take care of half a dozen families and loaned money to many others.

Shadows on the Rock was published in August of 1931. Another historical novel that compares the past with the present, the story is set in seventeenth-century Canada and tells of European men and women who struggle to adapt to life in the new world of North America as they try not to forget their lives in Europe. The book was well reviewed and became the most popular book in the United States during the next year.

By this stage in her writing career, Cather was generally regarded as an important American novelist, and major American magazines ran articles about her. *The New Yorker* did a profile of Willa, and *Time* magazine put her on its cover.

Cather was featured on the cover of *Time* magazine in its August 3, 1931 issue.

MEMORIES OF NEBRASKA AND VIRGINIA

One month after *Shadows on the Rock* was published, her mother died in California. While it was a relief to have her mother's long ordeal over, losing her was very painful. A few months after her mother's death, Cather organized a family reunion at Christmas in Red Cloud. The family gathering was a great success, and good therapy. Cather felt her mother's presence with the family during the holiday season. It was to be Cather's last visit to Red Cloud.

In 1932, Cather published a collection of three stories under the title *Obscure Destinies*. Cather used Nebraska as a setting in *Obscure Destinies*. The critics, pleased she'd returned to the plains locales, gave it rave reviews.

A NEW HOME

After five years of living in hotels with their belongings in storage, Cather and Lewis moved to a new apartment on Park Avenue on the east side of New York City. Once settled in, Cather's creative energy began to return, and she was ready to start working again. The new apartment was like a nest, sheltering her from worries over the economic distress in the United States, and signs from Europe of the possibility of another world war. She saw only a small circle of friends, in particular the Menuhins, a family of talented musicians she'd met in France in 1930.

In 1935, Cather learned that Isabelle Hambourg was suffering from an incurable kidney ailment. She was very upset over the news that her dear friend was so sick. Cather helped care for Isabelle while Jan Hambourg was on a concert tour. That same year, Cather's next book, *Lucy Gayheart*, was published. It was the story of a young music student who leaves behind her small Midwestern town and journeys to Chicago to study for a music career. The book deals with the theme of artistic growth and the price one has to pay to pursue a life in art.

Over the next few years, Cather lived quietly, going to concerts, socializing with friends, and answering letters from readers. She put together a collection of her previously published essays called *Not Under Forty*. With the publication of this book in 1936 came letters and telegrams from fans and friends, as well as more requests for interviews and speaking engagements. Cather was finding it more and more exhausting to answer these requests. Now sixty-three years old, her desire for quiet and privacy had grown much greater.

Prestigious Literary Honors

Along with the Pulitzer Prize and many honorary doctorates, Cather received a number of other prestigious literary honors, including the Howells Medal from the American Academy of Arts and Letters for *Death Comes for the Archbishop*, the Prix Femina Americaine—an international award—for *Shadows on the Rock*, and the gold medal for fiction from the National Institute of Arts and Letters, a prize of which she was particularly proud.

DIFFICULT DAYS

In the spring of 1937, Cather began work on a new book titled *Sapphira and the Slave Girl*. Cather wanted to write a book set in Virginia and use the true-life story of her grandmother Rachel Boak, the family housekeeper Aunt Till, and Till's daughter, Nancy. Cather made a trip to Back Creek to refresh her memories for the story.

In June of 1938, her brother Douglass died suddenly of a heart attack in San Diego, and in October Isabelle Hambourg died of kidney failure. Both were devastating losses for Cather, and she was very depressed. Then, in 1939, World War II began, and the news put Cather into an even deeper slump. For months, she could not write at all.

This photograph of Cather was taken in her New York City apartment in 1936.

Finally, the urge to create grabbed hold of her, and she began to work again on *Sapphira and the Slave Girl*. The creative process revived her spirits. Knopf published the novel on her birthday, December 7, 1940. Cather used all her Virginia childhood memories in the book, and the epilogue of the story is the reunion that occurred between Aunt Till and her daughter, Nancy, which Cather witnessed as a child. The dark, Gothic tale was almost unanimously praised by reviewers and was a huge commercial success. The book would be her last novel.

ENDINGS AND GOOD-BYES

Cather had pain from inflamed tendons in her hands and arms that hampered her writing, and she managed to write only two more stories and the beginning of another novel in the last six years of her life.

As the war ended in 1945, Cather was working on a story set in Nebraska called "The Best Years" that she planned to give as a gift to her brother Ross—a reminder of their life together when they were children in Red Cloud. She was getting ready to send it to Ross when she received word that he'd suffered a fatal heart attack.

Roscoe was the member of her family that Willa had been closest to, and his death broke something inside her. She'd now lost her parents, brothers Douglass and Ross, and best friend Isabelle Hambourg. She didn't care about writing anymore. At seventy-two, the emotional suffering of the last years had drained a lot of Willa's strength.

Finally, in the spring in 1947, some of Cather's old energy returned when she began thinking about writing again. She had some new ideas for stories. Cather started going out more, attending a few concerts, and even making plans for the summer. On April 24, her spirits were up and she was happy. At 4:30 P.M., she died suddenly of a stroke.

After her death, a collection of Cather's short stories, *The Old Beauty and Others*, was published in 1948 by Knopf. She left a literary legacy of seventeen books, more than sixty short stories, and numerous critical reviews, essays, and speeches. Her work has been translated into countless languages, including Japanese, German, Russian, French, Czech, Polish, and Swedish.

She is widely recognized as a major American writer and one of our country's best-known women writers. Cather wrote with passion and lyricism about the American land and its beauty; about women and the choices they make to fulfill their hopes and dreams; and about artists struggling to have the careers they dream of.

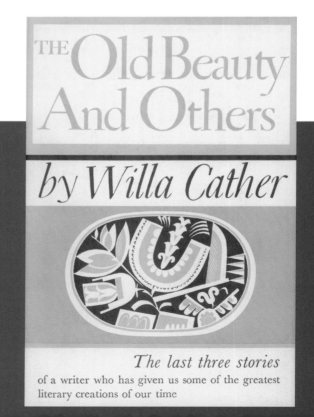

This is the original cover for *The Old Beauty and Others*, which was published after Cather's death.

Willa Cather is buried next to Edith Lewis in Jaffrey Center, New Hampshire. Carved on her gravestone is this sentence: "The truth and charity of her great spirit will live on in the work which is her enduring gift to her country and all its people." Below this is carved a quotation from her book, *My Ántonia*: "that is happiness; to be dissolved into something complete and great."

Honors Beyond Awards

Willa Cather has received many tributes beyond literary awards.

- **In 1962, she was the first woman voted into the Nebraska Hall of Fame, and was inducted into the Hall of Great Westerners in Oklahoma City, Oklahoma, in 1974, and into the National Women's Hall of Fame at Seneca Falls, New York, in 1988.**

- **In 1974, The Nature Conservancy purchased 610 acres (247 ha) of native grassland south of Red Cloud, and it was dedicated as the Willa Cather Memorial Prairie.**

- **A section of the University of Nebraska-Lincoln Botanical Garden and Arboretum pays tribute to her with The Cather Garden, a collection of native grasses, wildflowers, shrubs, and trees.**

- **In 2000, the International Astronomical Union named Asteroid No. 14969 after Willa Cather.**

Timeline

WILLA CATHER'S LIFE   WORLD EVENTS

1873 Cather is born on December 7 in Back Creek Valley, Virginia.

      United States experiences a financial panic.

1883 The Cather family joins Willa's grandparents William and Caroline Cather and her uncle George in Webster County, Nebraska.

1884 Cather's family moves to Red Cloud, a railroad town nearby.

1892 Cather's first short story, "Peter," is published in a Boston magazine.

      Ellis Island is opened in New York Harbor to receive immigrants.

1895 Cather graduates from University of Nebraska.

1896 Cather moves to Pittsburgh to edit *Home Monthly* magazine and writes reviews for *Pittsburgh Leader*.

1903 *April Twilights* is published.

1904 Ida Tarbell publishes *History of Standard Oil*.

1905 Cather's short story collection *The Troll Garden* is published.

1906 Cather moves to New York to work for *McClure's Magazine*.

1908 Henry Ford introduces the Model T automobile.

1912 *Alexander's Bridge* is published. Cather visits the Southwest for the first time.

1913 *O Pioneers!* is published.

1914 World War I begins.

1917 The United States enters World War I.

1918 *My Ántonia* is published.

World War I ends on November 11.

1920 Her short story collection *Youth and the Bright Medusa* is published.

1922 *One of Ours* published.

1923 She wins the Pulitzer Prize for *One of Ours*. *A Lost Lady* is published.

1925 *The Professor's House* is published.

1926 *My Mortal Enemy* is published.

1927 *Death Comes for the Archbishop* is published.

1929 Worldwide economic depression begins.

1930 Cather is awarded the Howells Medal of the American Academy of Arts and Letters for *Death Comes for the Archbishop*.

1931 *Shadows on the Rock* is published.

1932 Her collection of three short stories, *Obscure Destinies*, is published.

1933 Cather receives the Prix Femina Americaine for *Shadows on the Rock*.

1935 *Lucy Gayheart* is published.

1936 Cather's essay collection, *Not Under Forty*, is published.

1939 World War II begins.

1940 *Sapphira and the Slave Girl* is published.

1941 The United States enters World War II.

1945 World War II ends.

1947 Cather dies on April 24.

To Find Out More

SELECTED BOOKS BY WILLA CATHER

Alexander's Bridge. New York: Simon & Schuster, 1998.

April Twilights: And Other Poems. Murietta, CA: Classic Books, 1998.

Death Comes for the Archbishop. Lincoln: University of Nebraska Press, 1999.

A Lost Lady. Murietta, CA: Classic Books, 1998.

Lucy Gayheart. New York: Random House, 1995.

My Ántonia. New York: Houghton Mifflin Co., 1995.

O Pioneers! New York: Oxford University Press, 1999.

One of Ours. Murietta, CA: Classic Books, 1998.

Willa Cather on Writing: *Critical Studies on Writing as an Art*. Lincoln: University of Nebraska Press, 1988.

BOOKS ABOUT WILLA CATHER

Bohlke, Brent L., editor. *Willa Cather in Person: Interviews, Speeches, and Letters*. University of Nebraska Press, 1986.

Cooney, Blanche. *In My Own Sweet Time*. Swallow Press, 1993

Lewis, Edith. *Willa Cather Living: A Personal Record*. Bison Books Corp., 2000

Slote, Bernice. *Willa Cather: A Pictorial Memoir*. Lincoln: University of Nebraska Press, 1973.

ORGANIZATIONS AND ONLINE SITES

Willa Cather Archive
http://www.unl.edu/Cather/

Maintained by the University of Nebraska, this site provides links to Cather's writings, biographical information, bibliographies, full-text Cather works, and pictures.

Willa Cather
http://fp.image.dk/fpemarxlind/

This site provides a timeline of events in Cather's life, with links to more information.

Willa Cather
http://www.gustavus.edu/oncampus/academics/english/cather

This page provides links to information about Cather, including events, biography, quotations, and publications.

Willa Cather Pioneer Memorial and Educational Foundation
326 North Webster Street
Red Cloud, NE 68970
http://willacather.org/

This organization's online site provides information about Cather, the memorial, and Red Cloud.

A Note on Sources

Much of the material in this book comes from reading Willa Cather's own letters, interviews, speeches, and fiction writing. The majority of research was done through the Willa Cather Pioneer Memorial and Educational Foundation in Red Cloud, Nebraska, the Willa Cather Archive at the University of Nebraska, as well as book and archive material in libraries. The major book sources consulted include: *Willa Cather in Person: Interviews, Speeches, and Letters*, edited by Brent L. Bohlke; *Willa Cather Living: A Personal Record*, by Edith Lewis; *Willa Cather: A Reference Guide*, by Marilyn Arnold; *Willa Cather: A Literary Life*, by James Woodress; *Willa Cather: The Emerging Voice*, by Sharon O'Brien; *Willa Cather: A Pictorial Memoir*, by Bernice Slote; and *Willa: The Life of Willa Cather*, by Phyllis C. Robinson.

—Bettina Ling

Index

About the Author

Bettina Ling has been a writer, editor, and author of educational material for children for more than seventeen years. She has written over sixteen books for children and young adults, including biographies of Aung San Suu Kyi, Maya Lin, Mairead Corrigan and Betty Williams, and Jose Cansesco. For Scholastic Library Publishing, Ms. Ling has written two volumes in the Sea to Shining Sea series: *Wisconsin* and *Indiana*. Ms. Ling has loved and admired the work of Willa Cather since she first read *My Ántonia* and *O Pioneers!* in school.